The FREEDOM OF Forgiveness

ALLEN B. JACKSON

The Freedom of Forgiveness

3G Publishing, Inc.
Loganville, GA 30052
888-442-9637
www.3gpublishinginc.com

Reprinted: 3G Publishing, Inc., October, 2022

Copyright © 2022 by Allen B. Jackson

All rights reserved. No part of this book may be reproduced, copied, stored or transmitted in any form or by any means – graphic, electronic, or mechanical, including photocopying, recording, or information storage and retrieval systems without the prior written permission of Allen B. Jackson or Hope of Vision Publishing except where permitted by law.

Unless otherwise specified, all Scripture quotations in this book are from The Holy Bible, King James Version (KJV). Copyright 1982 by Thomas Nelson, Inc.

Cover Design: Hope of Vision Designs Cover Image: Google Images

Editor: Owerri Washington

Write the Author at:
Email: allenbjackson@hotmail.com
Website: www.allenbjackson.com

Also Follow me on social media: Allen B. Jackson on Facebook and Instagram. And subscribe to my You Tube channel @ Allen B. Jackson. For more information about special discounts for bulk purchases, please contact Email: allenbjackson@hotmail.com

ISBN 978-1-956382013

Printed in the United States of America

Endorsement

"Allen reveals in his personal life story how he confronts a tragic fork in the road and how it gives all of us a profound teaching on the power of forgiveness. Allen is a master at integrating the world of theology and psychology in his book. In using himself as the protagonist, he takes us on a personal journey of discovering that unforgiveness is a piercing thorn in the side of one's soul. Though the murder of his mother by his brother poses a seemingly insurmountable obstacle to get pass, Allen proves to us all that anything is possible through the power of forgiveness".

Dr. Ron Mercer, PHD, LMHC, NCC, Director of community services center for creative living and author of "Unspoken language of men" Coral Springs, Florida. *(Deceased)*

"When a deep injury is done to us, we never heal until we forgive."

NELSON MANDELA

The Freedom of Forgiveness

DEDICATION

Gloria Jean Jackson-Morris

February 11, 1949 – December 17, 1993

This book is dedicated to my hero and the strongest person I have ever known in my entire life: my mother, my friend and greatest supporter, Gloria Jean Jackson-Morris. Thank you for everything you taught me and especially for teaching me to always be strong and independent. I still remember the things you told me when I was a little boy. May you continue to rest in peace. I love you always and forever!

Rhonda Lowe

To my best friend and the only person that went through this tragedy with me. Thank you for your love and support when I felt all alone. Love you always!

Gabrielle Jackson

You are my princess, and you are the best daughter a dad could ask for. You bring so much joy to my life and you are my gift from God. I love you more than words can express.

Acknowledgment

I want to acknowledge and give my sincere heartfelt thanks to The Lowe family. And to the people that God eventually brought into my life after the tragedy of losing my mom. You all are friends that became my family. Willie and Juanita Creech, Beverly and Halam Batson, Elaine Stevens and Agnes "mommy" Joseph. And the entire Ark Church Family!

Table of Content

Chapter 1	**13**
My Family	
Chapter 2	**29**
December 17, 1993	
Chapter 3	**45**
Christmas Eve 1993	
Chapter 4	**69**
Time for Justice	
Chapter 5	**89**
Where Do I Go From Here?	
Chapter 6	**103**
The Letter	

Chapter 7 — 115

The Journey to Forgiveness

Chapter 8 — 125

What Forgiveness is and is Not

Chapter 9 — 135

Signs of Unforgiveness

Photo Album — 143

Contact the Author — 146

Prologue

One of life's greatest luxuries is freedom. Freedom gives a person the opportunity to be, to do and to have. When a person's freedom is taken away, they can no longer experience all that life has to offer. Often when a person loses their freedom, it's as a result of being incarcerated. But you don't have to be in a jail cell or sent off to prison to lose your freedom. I've learned through personal experience that allowing unforgiveness to linger, to lie dormant and unaddressed, will cause us to be imprisoned in our minds.

Unforgiveness is a prison. It takes away a person's emotional, mental and spiritual freedom, and according to extensive studies, unforgiveness can cause serious health issues. Just as criminals are locked away in prison, unforgiveness keeps us locked away in the prison of our minds and hearts and prevents us from living a free, productive, successful, and meaningful life. It has taken me twenty-one years to write this book, because forgiving and living in forgiveness is a journey.

Author's Notes

This is a work of nonfiction. Some names have been changed in order to respect and protect their privacy. While circumstances and comments depicted herein come from my recollection of them, this book is the best recollection of an event that changed my life forever.

Chapter 1

My Family

"STOP IT! STOP IT! STOP IT - GODDAMNIT! Leave him alone!" Our mother screamed at me.

"Why are you always taking up for him Mama?" I yelled back. "All he does is sit around and eat and sleep. He doesn't work, he doesn't help around the house and on top of everything, he steals money from you! All you do is baby him. He's a grown man."

Immediately my mother screamed back at me, "Watch your mouth! Who do you think you're talking to? He's my child, not yours!" She continued to scream.

And in good-ole-stubborn-Allen fashion I screamed back, "That's the problem Mama, you're treating a grown man like he's still a child."

It didn't matter what I said, my mother was always going to take up for Jeff no matter what or how wrong he was. This was just one of the many episodes of me and Jeff clashing. I had such a disdain and disgust for how lazy he was and how he would manipulate our mother. Our mother wasn't a stupid person, so I'm sure she was well aware that Jeff was a no good, lazy moocher. But she would always remind me by saying, "He's, my child." I was always left baffled at why she would take up for him and defend Jeff even in his wrongdoing.

One day I had just arrived at home from working two jobs only to find Jeff laying on the couch watching TV. The minute I saw him just casually laying there without a care in the world, I just lost it. I began screaming at him about how lazy and good for nothing he was and as usual, Jeff responded with a sarcastic comment and it just made my skin crawl - I just couldn't contain my anger with Jeff. It drove me up the wall to see him manipulate and use our mother the way he always did. Here he was a grown man, but he didn't work. He would mooch money off our mother almost every day. He would regularly have his friends over and they would run through our groceries as if they bought them. But again, my mother would let him get away with it. I felt the same way about his friends as I did about him, I considered them all losers. Not to mention the fact that some of his friends looked really shady which made me worry a lot about them being in our house around our mother. Sometimes my mind would wonder, and I would imagine them robbing, beating or doing something heinous to my mother.

The Freedom of Forgiveness

Jeff and I had a volatile relationship that would only worsen as time went on. All I wanted was for him to be a man, work and take care of himself. That night, like other nights after Jeff and I got into an altercation, I went to bed with a clinched fist and a cold heart. Every day, I started to resent Jeff more and more because I didn't like how he was treating our mother.

My days started around 4 a.m. I was working as a warehouse stock person by day, working 5 a.m. to 2 p.m. By night, I could be found cleaning bank buildings with my mom. I had started a janitorial cleaning business, so after leaving my day job, I would go home, get a quick nap, and head out around 6 p.m. to start cleaning several bank buildings that I sub-contracted from a general cleaning contractor.

Like so many little boys, my childhood dream was to become an NBA star. A close second had always been owning and operating my own business. The NBA didn't happen, so I settled for starting my own business. My mother was a maid all my life growing up, and she taught her three boys how to clean, along with many other things she felt we needed to know how to do for ourselves. As a kid, I always thought that my older brother and my younger brother would purposely put very little effort into their chores, leaving most of the cleaning and laundry for me to do, since I took pride in being clean. I was my mom's default "go-to" person when cleaning, doing laundry, or anything else that needed to be done, and "done right," as she would say to me when my brothers would not clean something up to her standards.

It frustrated me on many occasions, because I felt that if I could clean efficiently, so could they. But when I grew up, the training I had received made starting a cleaning business easy and effortless for me, not to mention the fact that I could do it with my role model and my hero, my mother.

During that period in my life, I was living at home with my mother, my stepfather Alvin, and my older brother Kevin. My younger brother Jeff, was in and out of the house, sometimes living with friends, other times moving back home. The relationship among us brothers was somewhat strained. For some reason we were never really close - well as kids we were close, but as we got older and became adults we grew apart for some reason. My older brother and I got along fairly well; we had our times when we argued as all siblings do, but overall, he and I were cool. Kevin was always the coolheaded one. Growing up I just remember that he always tried to avoid arguments. He was also the smartest one of us all. As I remember, Kevin always got the best grades from elementary school all the way into high school. I must admit, even though I was probably more popular than Kevin in school because I played sports, I was low-key jealous of how smart he was. Kevin was a good basketball player, but he never played on the school teams. On the other hand, I played on the little league, middle and high school basketball teams. I also played little league football

I was the big mouth kid in the family, while Kevin and Jeff were more on the quiet side. I was more outgoing and I never liked staying inside whenever I was home. I always wanted to be in the streets. You could always find me at the basketball court, the football field, hanging out with friends or hanging out with whoever my girlfriend was at the time. Growing up in my neighborhood wasn't easy because of the challenges we faced like drugs, crime, prostitutes, bullies and everything else that came with the previously mentioned elements. But as dangerous as our neighborhood was, I loved being in the middle of all the craziness. I was cool with most of the undesirables, but there were times when I wished we could move to a safer neighborhood. I can remember this one particular bully in our neighborhood, and I always prayed that he would not bother or try to bully me. He was merciless. He would just punch guys in the face for no reason and when the person fell to the ground, he would continue to humiliate them by kicking them and spitting on them.

Well, on one occasion, the neighborhood bully finally made his rounds to me. It was at the school bus stop when I was in middle school. I was a small kid growing up, in fact I was skinny and extremely little in stature. The biggest thing on me was my mouth. I think I was able to avoid most fights because I had such a good "talk game." I could talk myself out of almost anything. But not on this particular morning at the bus stop. My older brother and I rode different buses to school because I was still in middle school while my oldest brother Kevin was now in high school. Even though Kevin didn't like arguing and he was more a peacemaker, he was a lot taller and bigger than I was and he could fight if he had too. It was an unspoken thing among us as brothers that while we could not get along at times, we were not going to let anyone else bother one of us, or pick on one of us. This unspoken rule was something that Kevin took to heart more than Jeff and I.

Well, the day came that I would be finally bullied, I remember the fear I felt. I remember the embarrassment I felt, and I remember thinking to myself that if my brother Kevin was with me that he would not have just stood by and let me get bullied. That was one of the longest days of my life - it seemed like that day would never end. I couldn't wait to get home so I could tell Kevin what happened. I just knew if nothing else, I would feel better telling Kevin what happened to me. Kevin was a protective big brother in his own way. He never really vocalized how much he cared, but my younger brother Jeff and I knew that he would look out for us, and protect us the best way he knew how.

When I got home that day Kevin was already home because high school got out before middle school. When I walked into the door of our apartment from school, I didn't tell Kevin right away about what happened to me because he was watching television. He was a big television watcher, so I didn't bother him. I waited until we all had gone to bed, and I asked Kevin, "Are you asleep?" He immediately replied, "No." I then proceeded to tell him what happened to me earlier that day. After I was done telling Kevin about being bullied, strangely enough, he never responded. I was confused. Kevin didn't say one word, I got absolutely no response.

When we woke up the next morning, we all got dressed and ready to go to school. I was afraid because I didn't know what to expect. I didn't know if the bullying would be worse than it was the day before, not to mention that Kevin never said anything when I told him what happened. In Kevin's typical manner of handling things, because he wasn't the big talker that I was, he just walked to the bus stop with me. When we got to my bus stop the bully wasn't there yet, so Kevin just stood there next to me. He didn't say a word, he just stood next to me looking around. Finally, from a distance I could see the bully coming and so could Kevin. When the bully finally made it to the bus stop Kevin told me to hold his books. I didn't know what he was going to do. In fact, I was even scared for Kevin because this bully was just as big as he was, but maybe a little more masculine and bigger.

But Kevin walked up to him with no fear and told the bully that he better never mess with his little brother again or else he would have to deal with him. And just like that, the fight broke out. Kevin and the bully went at it. At first, I didn't know if I should jump in the fight and help Kevin, but it only took a few minutes for me to realize that Kevin didn't need my help. Kevin was handling this bully like a rag doll. I must admit that I was surprised. I had never really seen Kevin fight before. By the time some other kids broke up the fight I was standing there in shock. My brother had just kicked the neighborhood bully's ass and I was so happy, but more importantly, proud of my brother. Kevin left the bus stop and went to school without talking to me before he left. He just took care of business and left. Later when we both got home, we never really talked about the fight. I told Kevin, 'Thanks," and his response to me was, "Alright." All he said was, "Alright." From that day until this day, Kevin and I have never really talked about the fight, but I gained so much respect for Kevin from that fight. I never told him, but I did. That was just how it was in our household. No one really expressed feelings or emotions to each other.

My relationship with my younger brother Jeff, was a different story. Our relationship was more volatile. We would not only argue, but on occasion, we would physically fight. I got out of the Army in 1989 and returned home only to find out that my youngest brother Jeff was a homosexual. How times had changed! Back then, it seemed to me that being gay was embarrassing, and at the time, my ignorance of homosexuality caused me to be extremely troubled, and really agitated. In the late 70's and 80's homosexuality had a negative stigma attached to it, especially in the black community and particularly the hood. As kids in the hood, we were taught that being a homosexual was horrible. We made fun of "gays" as we called them and used derogatory names such as faggots and for lesbians, we used the term bull daggers. I couldn't tell you where these terms came from, I just used them because everyone else in the hood used them. The ignorance was passed on to me by my environment. At that time, we thought that homosexuality was a mostly white lifestyle, and because of this ignorance, I personally didn't accept or like gay people growing up. It was weird to me. So, when I found out that Jeff was gay, I was surprised because something that I hated had found its way into my family, and because of my ignorance and not understanding that lifestyle I treated Jeff as if he was sick in his mind. In my mind, no regular human being would want to be like that. This was the sole reason for Jeff and I having such a volatile relationship at this age and stage of our lives. I despised him for being gay and I wanted nothing to do with him.

It was also disturbing to discover that my brother was not working and seemingly uninterested in being employed. His idea of supporting himself was to mooch off my mom. Now the fact that my mom would secretly, and sometimes openly, give him money was troubling to me as well as my stepfather and my older brother. This issue kept us all at odds with my younger brother. In my opinion, I considered him to be a bum. He was very disrespectful to my mother in many ways that I would not tolerate.

The Freedom of Forgiveness

For example, he would argue and even curse at her at times. We were constantly at odds. Often, we would engage in physical fights, always initiated by me because it pained and angered me to see him use my mother and play on her emotions to get money from her. And, just like a mother, she always defended him and at times got angry at me for the way I treated my younger brother, even though it was all because I didn't like the way he would treat her. But they tell me that's a mother's love, and I will never understand a mother's love. She defended him, she would sneak money to him, and allowed him to live in the house even when my stepfather was adamantly against it.

Upon graduating from high school in 1985, I immediately left home and joined the U.S. Army. Leaving home was actually a little scary because that's all I ever knew. However, I knew that I had to get away from the neighborhood that I lived in because of all the bad influences of drugs, drug dealers, prostitutes, poverty and really poor living conditions. Growing up in the hood is a life of survival. Every day I was subject to violence and negative influences, so I knew that if I wanted to have some chance at life and not end up dead or in prison that I needed to get away. I had always had that dream of being an NBA star since I was pretty good at basketball, but I was a terrible student in school. I clowned around, skipped classes and ended up not graduating with my class and I had to attend an extra year of high school. And because I had no opportunities to attend college

The Freedom of Forgiveness

I decided to go into the Army. I specifically choose the Army because my uncle, one of my mother's brothers was in the Army at that time and he would tell us stories about his travel to Germany and other foreign places. It sounded so exciting to me, not to mention that he would also tell us about all the ladies he was involved with. So fun, travel and ladies, that was enough for me to make a decision to leave and join the Army. Growing up in the hood did not afford kids like me any real positive opportunities.

Before I graduated from high school, I entered into the Army delayed-entry program. This program allowed kids that were 18 years or older to take the military test during the school year and upon passing, to enlist without their parent's signature for permission if they were not 18 years old when they entered the program. After I passed the test, and I was accepted into the Army I told my mother what I had done. One day I remember just blurting it out to her, "Hey Ma, guess what? I joined the Army." I was kind of surprised at her response because my mother never held back her opinion about anything. She really didn't have much to say, but she did ask me, "Is this really something you want to do?" And I replied, "Yeah, it is. I gotta do something with my life or this neighborhood is going to eat me alive. I'm gonna end up in prison for selling drugs or dead." She responded, "OK," and went on about what she was doing. The only thing that would be hard was leaving my mother. We didn't have much of a family unit. My father was never in our lives

The Freedom of Forgiveness

and my mother struggled to take care of her 3 sons all by herself. In my mind I thought that going to the Army would also afford me an opportunity to help my mother out by sending her money to pay bills. I hated seeing my mother work 3 jobs to make a living and I hated the jobs she had. She worked as a maid in a hotel, a waitress in a diner and she ran errands on the weekend for rich, elderly white people, picking up their clothes from the cleaners, their groceries and medicines. So, for me, I felt like maybe I could send enough money back home to her to help relieve her from at least one of those jobs.

As my high school graduation drew closer, my mom and I never really talked any more about my decision to join the Army. I remember the day that the recruiter picked me up after I graduated from high school to take me to the airport. I asked him if my mother could ride with us and if he would bring her back home. He said yes, of course. When we arrived at the airport it was interesting because I was 18 years old, and I had never flown on an airplane a day in my life. I didn't have to do anything because my recruiter took care of everything and led my mom and I to my departing gate. As I waited to board my flight my mom and I just sat silently in our seats. We actually didn't talk at all. My mother just looked around the airport and I did the same thing. Finally, the airline employee came across the intercom informing us that the flight I was scheduled for was ready to board. This was really it. I was leaving home. I was really going into the Army. As I stood up, my mother stood up as well. She looked at me as if she wanted to say something, but the words just wouldn't come out her mouth.

My mom loved her boys more than anything in the world, but she never said the words. My mother wasn't the lovey-dovey type. She showed us that she loved us by taking care of us the best way she could. So, as we continued to stand there, I just grabbed her and hugged her tightly and I said to her, "Mama I love you." When I let her go and stood back, I noticed that she had tears in her eyes. She responded with these simple words. "Don't you get in no trouble OK?" I said, "OK" and I walked away feeling like maybe I was making a mistake by leaving home…but there was no turning back now.

As I sat on the plane heading to Ft. Leonard Wood, Missouri, I had a million thoughts running through my mind and almost all of them were about my mom. I just wondered would she be okay. I had never been away from her. When I arrived at my basic training station I was totally in a new world, and everything was so uncertain. But after 26 weeks of basic training and AIT school which was where I learned my trade, I graduated and entered into permanent duty status. The Army turned out to be everything my uncle had told me. I can truly say it exposed me to a life outside of growing up in the hood that I never dreamed of. When the time came for me to make a decision on my first duty station I chose Germany - solely because of the stories my uncle had told me about his time in Germany. This new adventure was something I needed and something that would prepare me for my life ahead.

I wrote my mother all the time and she would write me back immediately. I wrote to her about my experiences in this foreign country, my new friends that I had made who were from all different states back home and about my work. As we wrote each other, we never really talked about what was happening with her and my brothers. She would always write that everyone was doing fine. Most of the letters were from me sharing my adventures with her. She would tell me how proud she was of me and remind me to stay out of trouble.

About a year in the Army my mom wrote to me and told me that her and Alvin, her long-time live-in boyfriend had finally gotten married. I wasn't surprised, and I was happy for them. Alvin had been in our lives for quite some time and I knew my mother loved him. I never bothered to write my brothers or my stepfather Alvin, because my mom was really the only one I cared to write too. I can honestly say that my time in the Army probably saved my life in that if I had stayed home, I would have probably been another statistic going to prison or dead.

After serving my 4 years in the Army I decided not to re-enlist. I just felt like I needed to be home with my mom. So, I left the Army to go back home. I wasn't sure what life was like now back home, but

The Freedom of Forgiveness

I just needed to be there, so I returned home in 1989. December 17, 1993, would be a pivotal moment in my life that would change my life and my destiny forever. Though it would be the most painful experience in my life, eventually purpose was birthed out of it.

CHAPTER 2

DECEMBER 17, 1993

My normal routine was usually to go directly home, catch a quick nap, and get ready to head out to clean banks with my mom. But December 17, 1993, would be different. On this day, I didn't stick to my normal routine. I decided to go by a car dealership. I was in the market for a small pickup truck to use for the cleaning business. At the time I was driving a two - door hatchback Honda Accord. But I felt like it was time to get a more suitable vehicle, not to mention the fact that the cleaning business was going pretty well financially. Normally, whenever I made what I considered to be a big decision, I consulted my mother first. That would be especially important for something she was directly involved in, like the cleaning business. At the time, there was no apparent reason for me to break my normal routine, and in fact, after spending an hour or so looking at several small pickup trucks I told the salesman that I needed to go, and that I would be back with my mom to look again. So, I left the car lot and headed home, only to remember that I had a doctor's appointment. I rushed home to change clothes for my appointment. When I arrived home, my mom was up to her normal things, fiddling around the house.

As a child growing up, we always lived in apartments in bad neighborhoods. We never had our own house. So, now that we finally had our own house it was nice coming home seeing my mom doing little things around the house. She got great joy out of decorating and redecorating, hanging up pictures and what not. She was always finding little bargains at the thrift store on tables, chairs, curtains and throw pillows for the sofa chairs. She was also a chef in her own right. There wasn't anything she couldn't cook so it was normal to come home and always find her cooking something. She enjoyed the opportunity to finally be a homeowner at this stage in her life. Especially considering the fact that she grew up extremely poor in a small town in Georgia and never had a home. And so, to have her own home was a dream come true for her and she created a very homey and comfortable environment in the house. She wasn't much of an outside person, so the yard and other outside projects were left to my stepfather. However, she would give my stepfather outside projects that she wanted done. She was truly a homebody and loved every aspect of it. I walked into the door and everything was normal. But for some reason which I can't explain, I asked her if she had seen Jeff, and she told me that he had just left, and that I had just missed him.

The Freedom of Forgiveness

"Did you give him money?" I asked her with an attitude. My mother gave me her classic response, "Mind your own business; he's my child," and walked away. My stop at the car dealership had made me miss my brother's visit. No doubt, I thought, he had come by with some of his good for nothing friends to get money from my mother. I would later find out that his visit to the house that day had ended in a heated argument between him and my mother, but that didn't mean she would entertain me and my disdain for him. It's funny, looking back, I never did get to that conversation about the truck I was considering purchasing. Whenever Jeff's name came up in conversation with my mom it was always hard to get back to a normal conversation. So, I showered, got dressed, and headed out to the podiatrist. As I was leaving, I told my mom about my appointment and that I would be back in time to head out to clean the banks.

My mom would say something to me that I didn't pay any attention to that day, but it rang loud in my mind years later. As I was walking out the door, my mom said to me, "OK, I'm tired. I'm going to lay down and get some rest. Just wake me up when you get back." I had no idea this would be the last time I saw my mother and that those would be the last words I would hear from my mother's lips.

After seeing the doctor, I headed back home to get ready to go clean the banks with my mom. I took the quickest way, so that I would have a few min-

The Freedom of Forgiveness

utes to relax before heading out to work. As I drove home everything was normal. I don't remember what music I was listening to, but everything else was normal. Normal traffic flow, normal weather and a normal overall feeling. However, as I approached the neighborhood that we lived in, things were not normal at all. Things were actually quite abnormal. To start, as I turned into our neighborhood, I saw police cars all over the place. I don't think I had ever seen so many police cars at one time in one place, and all I could think was that something bad must have happened. As I continued to drive, I also noticed a few paramedic trucks, so now I was thinking, "Wow, something really bad has happened!" And just like that, my normal day had turned into something chaotic and crazy. Now, the sky seemed grey and dreary. There was no more music playing in my ears and that normal overall feeling had quickly disappeared. As I continued to drive up the street going into my neighborhood, a police officer standing in the road was pointing, and directed me to pull over. I rolled down my window, and the police officer asked me where I was going. I told him that I was going home and that I lived on the street they had blocked off. The police officer asked me for my ID. I gave my ID to him and I noticed a weird look on his face as he asked me to get out of the car. At this point all kinds of thoughts were racing through my mind.

Why was he asking me to get out of my car? Why did he have this weird look on his face after he looked at my driver's license? And where was he

The Freedom of Forgiveness

taking me? As I got out of the car, the police officer asked me to walk with him. At this point my heart was pounding as if it was going to jump out of my chest. I can still remember every step.

I could literally feel the vibration of the officer and my footsteps as our feet hit the pavement walking towards our house. While it was only about 20 yards from where I parked to where our street began, it seemed like one of the longest walks of my life. It was like everything was moving in slow motion at this point. I could sense everything. Everything was heightened in my body. Now the sounds of the sirens, the many officers standing around talking and the police radios were all clear in my ears. As we turned to walk onto my street, I noticed that all of this commotion was centered on our house. Yellow tape was stretched around the front of our yard. I could see my aunt and my stepfather in the driveway, looking distraught.

As the police officer and I got closer to the house, it became hard for me to breathe. My breaths got shorter, and it felt as if something extremely heavy had dropped on my chest. I got so nervous that my body began to shake. As I walked up to the driveway where my stepfather and my aunt stood, they were both looking at me and they were both crying and sobbing uncontrollably. I couldn't take it anymore; I quickened my steps to a little jog.

The Freedom of Forgiveness

"What happened, what happened?" I asked. They just looked at me as they were both shaking their heads. Neither one of them could get any words out. I asked again and again, what happened. Getting no immediate answer from either one of them I started screaming and crying out, "Where is Mama? What happened to Mama?" Finally, my stepfather turned to me with tears running down his face and flooding his cheek bones and said these words to me, "Allen, Glo is gone. She's gone Allen! Glo is dead!" as he grabbed his head with both of his hands. Glo was the name we affectionately called my mom, which was short for Gloria.

At that moment, I was flooded with emotions. I was overwhelmed. I screamed at the top of my lungs, "Noooooooooo, please God, noooooo!"

I ran toward the walkway leading to the front door, but immediately a couple of police officers grabbed me and told me I couldn't go in. It started with just a couple of officers holding me, but then a few more officers joined in and started grabbing my shoulders, my arms and holding me around my waist. I tried to pull away from them and go inside, but they continued to hold me and restrain me, telling me I couldn't go in. I didn't want to hear what they were saying. All I wanted to do was see my Mama. As I tussled with the officers, I felt my body getting weaker and weaker, but I couldn't stop, I had to see my Mama. I felt like she needed me. I could

The Freedom of Forgiveness

hear one officer saying, "Don't hurt him, just hold him but he can't go inside the house."

"But why? My Mama needs me." This is what was going through my mind as the officers held me. I just kept screaming, "I just want to see my Mama!" I started thinking to myself these officers just don't know how much my Mama means to me and how bad I needed to see her.

"Let me go please, please let me go!" I started screaming but the officers wouldn't give in to my request. "If only they would just let me go. If only they understood the pain I was feeling." At some point my body went lifeless as I dropped to the ground, screaming, "Mama, Mama, Mama! Oh God, my Mama! I want to see my Mama! I want to see my Mama!" I fell to the ground and just sobbed, "Mama, Mama, Mama, Oh God my Mama!"

The next thing I knew was that I woke up lying on a gurney in the back of one of the paramedic trucks. I immediately jumped up, asking to see my Mama. The paramedics tried to tell me in the most sensitive and thoughtful way that my mom was dead. I could see it in their faces, but there was no way to tell me that my mother was dead that would have been OK with me.

I asked them to let me out of the truck and they did. I ran over to my stepfather and my aunt standing in the driveway. By this time, my oldest brother

Kevin had arrived, and he was crying uncontrollably. I started to cry and scream again. The pain that permeated my body was indescribable. It felt like someone had torn my chest open and snatched my heart out of my body. But all of a sudden, in the midst of my pain, my tears and the hurt, it hit me:

Why was my younger brother Jeff not there? Where was he?

"Where is Jeff?" I asked my aunt and my stepfather. "Has anyone talked to him or seen him?" They told me they couldn't reach him because they didn't know where he was. And immediately, as though I had seen it myself, I screamed, "Jeff did this!" Over and over again I screamed, "Jeff DID THIS!" My aunt and my stepfather looked at me in disbelief.

"Jeff did this," I said it again. "He killed Mama, I know he did this."

I didn't care who heard me and I didn't care if anyone believed me or not. I ran up to one of the police officers. "My brother did this," I told him. The officer looked at me in confusion and tried to calm me down. "You're upset," he said. "We'll find the person or persons that did this." The officer hugged me around my shoulders and walked me down the sidewalk a little. He turned and faced me, and he told me my mom had been shot in her head at point-blank range as she slept. He went on to tell me that there was no evidence of a break-in, a robbery, or even a tussle. She was laying on her back as if asleep, with a pillow in her arms. I screamed out again, "Jeff did this!" The officer tried to console me, but after hearing what he had just told me for some strange reason, deep in my soul, I knew that my brother Jeff had murdered our mother. I told the police officer, "I'm going to find him and kill him." Something had shifted in me. In that moment, I had moved from what seemed to be deep grief to an extreme state of rage, such as I had never felt before. As I continued to scream that "I was going to kill Jeff," the detectives in plain clothes came over to me and told me to stop saying that I was going to kill him.

They told me that I was going to get myself in trouble and possibly be detained. But I couldn't calm down. I was overtaken with anger and rage. I didn't care what they threatened to do to me at that point. So, I kept saying it. Not only did I say it again and again, but I really meant it. All I could think about was killing Jeff. Standing there, I made it my mission in life to kill my younger brother, to make him pay for what he had done. I will probably never be able to explain why or how I knew he had done it. Just like every other family, we had our issues, but nothing that I could point to that could justify the way I felt.

Even now looking back, it's still surreal and unbelievable that he would have done this. But I just knew. I managed to calm myself down at some point and I asked one of the officers again to let me see my

The Freedom of Forgiveness

Mama one last time. The tears started pouring out and rolling down my face like a waterfall. "Please, please," I started begging the police officers. "I want to see my Mama, I want to see my Mama," as I fell to my knees. At that point one of the officers kneeled down and started to console me. He helped me get back on my feet and he walked me over to the side and told me that the coroner had taken her body away while I was unconscious in the ambulance.

"Trust me," he gently said, "You didn't need to see her the way we found her. Just remember her the way you last saw her." His words, "remember her the way you last saw her" caused me to freeze. My mind immediately went back to earlier that day when I was leaving the house and my mother told me she was tired and that she was going to lay down and get some rest. She told me to wake her up when it was near time for us to head out to do the cleaning. She told me she was tired and that she was going to get some rest. Her words repeatedly echoed in my mind. I know she meant at the time that she was physically tired, but was that God's way of allowing me to understand that my mom was also tired from all that she had been through in life? Was that a sign? Did she know it was her time to go? It was all I could think to myself. I stood there for a few minutes in a daze.

Suddenly, the sound of police cars starting their engines caused me to come back to reality. Now I started thinking, "Why? Why would Jeff do this?

The Freedom of Forgiveness

What happened when Jeff came home after I left?" I went back to the plain-clothes detective.

"I know my brother did this."

"Why are you so sure," he asked me. "Do you know something we don't know?"

I had no answer for him. "I just know Jeff did this, that's all I can tell you. I just know he did it." I started looking around. The detective said, "Here's my card. If you need me, call me." Then he said, "If you find Jeff—call me."

I looked around again and realized darkness had set in. The day was over. It seemed like we all had been there for days, but it had only been for hours. My stepfather, my aunt, and my older brother were still standing in the driveway. As I walked back over to them, another detective was telling them that the house was now a crime scene, and we could not go into it until the house was released.

My heart skipped a beat when I heard his words. The place that was our home was now a crime scene. "A crime scene," I thought to myself. You never think certain things will happen to you. I mean I had seen things like this on the news, but to be actually living it myself, it was just chilling and unbelievable. Because our house was now a crime scene this meant that my stepfather, my oldest brother and myself were displaced. And so, it hit me, where are we going to go? As soon as I started thinking about where we were going to go, my aunt told us that we could all come and spend the night at her house. I'm not sure if my stepfather and oldest brother went, but I didn't. I went into my own world. As I stood there in the driveway, my anger and fury returned tenfold. The feeling of hate was taking over my entire being.

"I'm going to find Jeff and I'm going to kill him," I said it out loud enough for them all to hear. My aunt pleaded with me. "No, Allen that's not the answer. Killing him won't bring Glo back. No more killing, please no more killing," my aunt said as she began to sob.

"And how do you even know for sure that he did this?" She asked me. I could not explain it, but I told her repeatedly, "I just know that he did it."

But bringing my mom back was not my goal at that point. My goal in life was no longer to be a successful businessman, but to find Jeff and kill him, just like he had killed our mother. As the police cars drove off, I started walking to my car thinking.

Where was he? Where should I start looking? Who was he with?

The Freedom of Forgiveness

I knew nothing of his friends, their addresses or where they lived or where they hung out so I had no idea how I would find him. As I got into my car, I decided to get a hotel room for the night and to try and sort things out. I drove until I came to the first hotel, and I checked into a room. As I walked to my hotel room, I started to think about how I was going to kill my younger brother. I didn't want him to die immediately, I wanted him to hurt and suffer first. As I opened the door of the hotel room, I looked at my watch, and by this time it was after midnight.

As I sat on the bed in the hotel room, my thoughts went wild. I started thinking about how Jeff could have done such a terrible thing. I started wondering why again. What would make Jeff murder our mother? It just didn't make any sense. And did my mom suffer? I laid back on the bed. How could I find my younger brother? For the next couple of hours my emotions vacillated between sadness and anger, hopelessness and fury. This was the longest night of my life.

From time to time, in between the thoughts of fury and anger, I would doze off to sleep. Every time I woke, I looked at my watch and thought this was going to be one of the longest nights of my life. Time was moving so slow. I turned on the TV. The lead story for the late-night local news was my mother's murder. I turned the TV off and the tears came rushing down my face again and I quickly fell back into my rage. I was screaming "Mama" so

The Freedom of Forgiveness

loud it was a wonder that the hotel staff at the front desk didn't come running to my room. I screamed until I couldn't scream anymore, and I cried myself to sleep. Only this time I had fallen asleep for a couple of hours. All of a sudden, my beeper went off. I looked at it, but I didn't recognize the number displayed. Who would be messaging me in the wee hours of the morning? I dialed the number back from the hotel room phone. When the phone stopped ringing, the voice of my younger brother came through the phone loud and clear.

"Allen, Allen! This is Jeff."

For a second, I was speechless. I was in shock. I literally froze up. But I quickly snapped out of that daze, and I screamed into the phone, "Where are you? Where the hell are you?"

"I didn't do it! I promise I didn't do it Allen!" He yelled.

I screamed louder. "You're a liar! Yes, you did! I'm going to find you and when I do, I'm going to kill you just like you killed Mama."

Jeff began to cry. He then said, "I don't know what happened Allen, I didn't do it." His crying meant nothing to me. And why was he crying anyway? Were his tears, tears of remorse? Was he hurting because our mother was dead? Were they tears of fear because I had threatened to kill him? My rage continued as I screamed and cursed at him.

"Where the hell are you? You're a fucking liar, you killed Mama."

He replied, "I can't tell you Allen, I can't tell you."

And then he just kept saying over and over, "I didn't do it, I didn't do it!" as his sobbing got louder and louder. I didn't want to hear what he was saying, I just wanted him to tell me where he was. He asked me to stop screaming at him and to stop cursing at him, but I couldn't get my rage under control.

"Fuck you!" I said to him. "You are a dead man!" I screamed into the phone.

He didn't say anything else. It's as if he just dropped the phone by his side so that he didn't have to hear my rage anymore. "I know you're still on this phone," I screamed again and suddenly the phone went silent, and then all I could hear was a dial tone. He had hung up the phone. I quickly redialed the number in my beeper and the phone just rang and rang. I'm sure it was a pay phone. The call left me with so many questions in my mind. Where did he call me from? Why was he crying? Was he telling the truth that he didn't do it? Why did he call me? What was I going to do now? Should I just go to my

The Freedom of Forgiveness

car and start driving around hoping to find him? I had no idea where he was, and I had no idea where to even start looking. I just sat there on the bed, more anxious and angrier as ever. I knew I wouldn't be able to fall back to sleep after his phone call. So, I just sat on my hotel bed, sobbing at times until the sun came up.

Chapter 3

CHRISTMAS EVE

It was the day before Christmas, and my hero, my role model, my mother had been murdered, and I knew my younger brother had done it. As I laid in bed looking up at the ceiling, I just felt lost. I felt alone. It was Christmas Eve and that meant nothing to me now. It used to be a day that was filled with excitement and anticipation, but now it was filled with anger, hurt, grief and uncertainty. I barely slept and all I could think about was where I could find Jeff. My mind drifted off and I started thinking about how things were going to be now that the heart and soul of our little family was gone. I started thinking about how Christmas would never be the same again for the rest of my life because the person who really made Christmas, Christmas, was gone.

Like for so many other mothers, Christmas was my mother's favorite holiday. She would always start decorating the day after Thanksgiving, and her decorations were always on point. She never missed a detail when it came to decorating the entire inside of the house and the outside. She would always turn on her favorite Christmas blues music, pour a glass of her Hennessey and coconut milk that she liked, and she would just bask in decorating. I would help her from time to time, but she really didn't like any help because she wanted everything to be perfect and done a certain way. That was my mother, she was the type of person that would rather do things the way she wanted them done the first time rather than have to go behind me or anyone else and do things over. The highlight of the decorations was her Christmas tree. When I was a kid, we really didn't have any money, so my mother would buy a small, cheap fake Christmas tree from K-Mart. Now by this time we weren't rich, but we had at least gotten to a place where we could actually afford a real tree, a big real tree. Oh, the smell of the pine would fill the house and my mother always saved the tree for last to decorate because it was the crown jewel and the climax of the decorations. Once the tree was done, that meant that Christmas decorations were complete.

I continued to daydream and think about how in the world would Christmas ever be the same. I mean, like even the count down until Christmas day. My mom would hide her gifts for us in her bedroom closet because we were all notorious for making little, small rips in the wrapping paper in our efforts to try and figure out what our gifts were. Then there was Christmas day dinner which started sometimes two nights before Christmas. My mother would prepare and pre-cook the food because all she wanted to do on Christmas day was eat. I would always hang around her in the kitchen and act as her official taste tester. The pride my mother took in cooking her Thanksgiving and Christmas dinners was serious business. Everything had to be just right. I liked being her taster. Spoon after spoon and fork after fork, the food kept coming. The collard greens, the yams, the potato salad, the stuffing, the corn bread, the baked beans, the green beans, the turkey, the ham, the white rice and gravy and the black-eyed peas were all our favorites. I mean I was literally full for a day or so after tasting all of the food. She would always say to me, "Does it need anything else? Is the flavor good?" And even though I would give her the thumbs up, she would always say, "I'm going to add a little bit more of this or that." She wanted the dinner to be grand and she loved our after-dinner compliments.

Now, while I really liked tasting the food, the highlight for me was when she would start baking. Oh My God!! The different kind of cakes, the sweet potato pies, the lemon meringue pie and other sweets were to die for. I loved licking the spoon of the pies and cakes. My favorite was the Sweet Potato pie batter. I could honestly eat a bowl of it by itself. And Oh, Christmas day! My mother would get up bright and early with the birds. We would all be awakened to the soulful Christmas music of some of her favorite singers like Nat King Cole, Al Green, Sam Cooke and the list went on and on. Regardless of all the food that she had prepared, she would always cook a

Christmas breakfast. It wouldn't be anything major or heavy, just something to hold us over until it was time for the grand Christmas dinner. After Christmas breakfast we would all take our showers and get dressed. My mother would finally bring out her gifts for us and put them under the tree. When she finally put our gifts under the tree the look on her face said "mission accomplished." She felt good about keeping us in suspense. And now that the gifts were under the tree, Christmas day had officially started.

My mother would send us out for quick errands to the store for things like ice, more beer, alcohol and more plastic spoons and forks. While she loved cooking, she wasn't crazy about washing dishes. When we finally made it to the dinner table it was as if we were in Heaven. The dinner table was decorated like a grand palace, the Christmas music was playing in the background and the food was spread out on the table. All that was left was to pray and dig in. After dinner it was always a sight to see. Everyone's belly was full, and all of the remains of our plates were front and center. Now that dinner was over it was time to open gifts. We had no specific order, we would just randomly start opening our gifts. Gift after gift brought on different responses. Most times, the response was excitement and joy, but every now and then someone would get or give a dud gift and the expression was obvious…and in Glo-fashion, my mother would always shout out, "Be thankful for what you got, there's people in other countries that don't have anything, not even a roof

The Freedom of Forgiveness

over their heads." That was my mother. She would always remind us to be thankful because things could always be worse. As Christmas day continued it consisted of us watching some basketball which my mother loved. After a couple of drinks, she was ready for her basketball. She would scream at the players on the TV and curse at them as well. It was our comedy and Christmas entertainment. To see the smile on my mother's face and to hear her laughter and silliness was the only gift I really needed. As Christmas day came to an end, my brothers and I would head out to hang with girlfriends and friends. Something was always happening Christmas night around the city and after a day of good eating and fun I was ready to hang out.

How would we continue these traditions without Glo? None of us could cook to the degree that she cooked. All I could think about was the void that now existed in our lives that nothing and no one would be able to fill. Reality was sinking in. But despite the pain and uncertainty, it was a beautiful day in sunny Fort Lauderdale, Florida. The sky was blue and clear, and the clouds seemed white as ever. The contrast was crazy. In all of this beautiful weather I was dealing with the ugliest thing I would ever have to deal with in my life; the death of my mother and the reality that my younger brother was the one who murdered her.

It was now seven days after the murder of my mother, I was still living in the hotel, and I hadn't

The Freedom of Forgiveness

heard much from the police. I wasn't able to contact Jeff and he never reached out to me again after that night I threatened to kill him. Maybe I should have tricked him into believing that I believed him just to find out where he was. Maybe I should have played along with his story. Maybe I should have just calmly listened to him and been understanding so that he wouldn't have felt so threatened by me and maybe he would have told me where he was.

Looking back, that probably would have landed me in prison for life because all I could think about was killing him. I wanted him to die so badly that it controlled my mind, my every thought and every emotion I had. It was time for me to leave the hotel. It was time for me to try to find a way to function even though my life would never be the same again. I had a hole in my heart that no other person would ever be able to fill.

As I prepared to leave the hotel room, the phone rang. It actually startled me a little. "Who was calling me?" I thought to myself. I slowly walked over to the phone. I wasn't sure if I wanted to answer it or not. And then it hit me. I had paged the detective at some point during the night and given him the number to the hotel I was staying in. Was it him? Was it Jeff? I slowly picked up the phone and it took me a few seconds to say, "Hello."

"Allen, my man," the voice said. It was the detective. "I have some good news and I have some bad news," he said. "Which do you want first?" I replied to him, "At this point it really doesn't matter."

"Well, the good news is that we have the person who killed your mother." My heart dropped and my mouth suddenly became extremely dry. My body froze. This was great news but I honestly wasn't prepared for this.

"What? Oh really?" I said. I was kind of speechless. And before he could tell me who it was, I just knew it was Jeff.

"Yes, that's the good news," he said. "But the bad news is that your suspicion was correct, the person who murdered your mother is your younger brother. Jeff did it."

There was a long pause. I stood still for a moment, overwhelmed and flooded with mixed emotions. On one hand I already knew he did it, but on the other hand, to actually hear it—I just wasn't prepared. The reality was overwhelming. I got silent.

"Mr. Jackson, are you still there?"

"Yes," I said. "I'm still here." I was trying to compose myself. "Yes, I'm here."

I took a deep breath. "Where is he? What happened? I closed my eyes as the detective started

The Freedom of Forgiveness

telling me the story. It's almost as if I was there in the room when it happened but I couldn't stop Jeff. It was as if I had been transported back in time:

My imagination took me back to that day. In my mind I saw Jeff approaching my mother's bedroom door. He knocked timidly as if he knew she was asleep and he didn't want to wake her, but he wanted it to be loud enough for her to hear his knock if she wasn't in a deep sleep. When our mother didn't answer his knock, he knew that she was asleep. He put his ear to the door and he could hear her snoring.

He stood at the door for a few minutes with the gun in his hand. Whatever happened earlier caused Jeff to be angry and he continued standing at her door with an angry look on his face. He slowly turned the doorknob. As he turned the doorknob, he started to open the door. As he opened the door, he saw our mother fast asleep laying on her back and gripping a pillow which was laid over her stomach. After he opened the door just enough where he could tip toe in the room, he slowly walked over to the side of our mother's bed with the gun hanging down by his side. When he reached her bedside, he just stood there for a few minutes just looking at our mother as she was peacefully sleeping. And all of a sudden, he raised the gun up and pointed it at our mother's temple area of her face. His hands began to shake, and his eyes were red with anger. He stepped closer to her head as if he wanted to make sure he didn't miss. All of a sudden, a loud bang went off and Jeff stood there in shock. He had pulled the trigger. He fell to his knees for a minute with the gun still in his hand. And suddenly he stood up and ran out of the room.

The detective was talking but I was in a twilight zone.

"Allen, Allen are you still there?"

My voice cracked as I said, "Yes, I'm still here."

The detective started telling me that earlier that Christmas Eve morning Jeff had turned himself in and confessed to shooting our mother. He said that he and my mother had gotten into a heated argument, and he went into one of the bedrooms and waited until she had gone back to sleep. When he was sure she was asleep, he opened her bedroom door, stood next to her bed, and at point-blank range, he pulled the trigger.

Tears ran down my face as I listened. I felt hopeless, sad and hurt all over again. As I continued to listen to the detective, he continued telling me that they had recovered the gun from the bedroom Jeff slept in. He had hidden it under his bed.

"Now that he's turned himself in and we have the gun, you and the rest of your family are free to move back into the house." I said, "Thank you, sir," and I hung up the phone. As I walked out of the hotel room, it was as if I was still in the twilight zone. I knew Jeff had done it, but now, having confirmation, a million questions seemed to race through my mind all over again.

Why did I know he had done it? What did they argue about that made him so angry that he would do this? And why hadn't my mother locked her bedroom door before laying down to sleep, knowing how Jeff would often come in and out, stealing things and parading his friends around the house and who knows what else? As I reached the counter to check out of the hotel, the receptionist's voice snapped me out of my trance.

"How was your stay, sir?" I blinked. If only she knew why I was there. I wondered if I should tell her why I was there. But I simply replied, "It was good." Before I reached my car in the hotel parking lot, I used a phone booth and I called my stepfather because I figured he had been contacted by the detective and he was probably at the house by now. When he answered the phone, he said, "You were right, it was Jeff."

I replied, "I know, the detective called me."

"Yes, and he told me he was going to call you. That's why I didn't try to call you. We are clear to be in the house again, are you on your way home?"

The Freedom of Forgiveness
"Yes, I'm on my way."

But could we really call our house a home again? It was still a crime scene in my mind. And I definitely didn't consider it home anymore. I was not ready at that moment to walk into that house. I didn't know what to expect; I didn't know what I would see that would cause more pain and hurt. I didn't know if my stepfather had cleaned up anything. I didn't know if I would see blood anywhere in the house or anything that would take me back to the horrible day my mother was murdered. So instead of going directly home I drove around for a couple of hours. Here it was Christmas Eve, and I didn't feel anything but sorrow and pain.

Christmas trees and Christmas decorations could be seen everywhere I turned. Families were preparing their dinners and family members were coming into town from near and far. There was a festive vibe in the air, but there was no reason for joy in my heart, and there would be no cheer in my house on this Christmas, and for many more to come. So, I started driving in the direction of our house. As I turned into our neighborhood and then on to our street, I started having flashbacks. The scene started replaying in my mind. It was as if I was reliving what happened all over again. Tears started running down my face. I didn't know what to expect upon arriving at the house. When I pulled up to the house and parked in the driveway, I just sat in the car for a few minutes, but it seemed like I sat in the car for days. I turned the car off and wiped the tears from my face. "I have to be strong," I thought to myself. As I got out of my car, I saw pieces of the yellow tape that the police used to rope off the house lying in the yard. I got out of the car and walked up to the front door. As I reached to open the door, I could see the black dust that the police used to look for fingerprints. It was all around the area of the doorknob. As I was about to enter the house, my heart began to race. Was I ready for what I would see inside? I thought for a minute maybe it was all a dream. A bad nightmare of some sort. Maybe when I opened the door my mom would be walking by on her way into the kitchen and asking me if I was hungry because she made one of my favorite dishes, her amazing Shepherd's pie. Maybe she would be laying in the den watching her soap operas. It didn't matter to me what she would be doing, I just wanted her to be there.

As I held the doorknob and before I could turn the knob, it swung open. My stepfather had heard my car pull up and had come to greet me. It wasn't my mom. She wasn't there. She was really dead. And I would never see her again. At that moment I would have given anything in the world to hear her voice again. To hear her laugh again. To even hear her argue with me again. I just wanted to see her again!! I walked in, we hugged each other, and we both began to cry. I could feel the hurt in his heart and I'm sure he could feel the hurt and pain in my heart.

The Freedom of Forgiveness

After we got ourselves together, I asked him, "Where's Kevin?" He said he didn't know. As I walked into the house, I purposely looked away from my mother's closed bedroom door. I went into the den and my stepfather followed me. I asked him, "Have you gone into the bedroom?" He said, "Yes." He told me there was some blood everywhere on the bed, the sheets and on the carpet that needed to be cleaned. All of a sudden in the midst of all this uncertainty, my cleaning mindset kicked in, but only partially. "I'm not going in there," I told my stepfather. "But let's get to cleaning the rest of the place."

We cleaned until night set in. I don't know how my stepfather did it. I saw him taking large garbage bags into the room and once he filled them, he tied them up and sat them outside of the bedroom door. I thought to myself, we should just go and put these bags in a garbage can in the back yard and burn them. And even though I couldn't go in the bedroom I realized that my stepfather would have to sleep in the room at some point. I didn't see how he was going to do it. At times while he was cleaning, he would come out to get more cleaners or bags and I could see tears running down his cheeks. All the while, we didn't talk much, if any at all. Most of our attention was dedicated to the task at hand – cleaning the home and trying to get back some kind of normalcy. At some point the phone started ringing. It was kind of startling to me. Was it the detective again? Did I want to answer it or let my stepfather answer it? I was near the phone, so I decided to answer it. I paused for a second and then I said, "Hello." It was Kevin. He wanted to know what was the latest about everything. He started asking me had I spoken to the detective yet and at that moment I gave him the news about Jeff and told him everything. He started sobbing and of course it made me start crying. Through my tears I just started telling him to come home. He continued crying and told me he was on his way. As soon as I hung up with him the phone rang again almost immediately. I thought to myself, "Who was this?" Of course, this was before caller I.D., so I had no idea who it was. I answered the phone cautiously.

"Hello," the voice said. "Is this you Allen?"

I recognized that it was the detective and I replied.

"I'm just calling to check on you guys," he said. "Even though the circumstances are bad, I want to wish you guys a Merry Christmas. I have no idea what it feels like for you guys, but I just wanted to check on y'all."

I said, "Thank you, I appreciate your call." I wished him a Merry Christmas as well and I told him I had to go. But when I hung up the phone, I said to myself, "Merry Christmas? I will never have another Merry Christmas again in my life." Christmas was all about family and the most important person in our family was gone. No one would ever be able to

The Freedom of Forgiveness

replace my mom. My mom made Christmas special. Her decorations, her Christmas music and the aroma of her Christmas dinner would never happen again. She was irreplaceable. Honestly, I didn't see myself ever celebrating Christmas again in my life. How could I, without my mother? For me Christmas no longer had any meaning and I felt as if it was just another day. But there we were, trying to move on. Trying to regain some kind of normalcy. And just like that the tears started streaming down my face again. My stepfather came out of the room and asked about the phone call. I told him Kevin called and was on his way home and that the detective called to check on us and wish us a Merry Christmas. He said, "That was nice of him," and we continued cleaning. Finally, later in the night, my older brother, Kevin came home. When he walked in the house, we all started to cry again. I knew that we all had a long road ahead of us.

Somehow, someway, we had to pick up the broken pieces and live. Glo would want nothing less. We had to move on and live, but how? How would we live without the centerpiece of the family? For the remainder of the night, there wasn't much said among the three of us. At some point, we all went to our rooms. For a moment, I was curious to see if my stepfather would sleep in the bedroom that he had shared with my mom for years. Perhaps he would sleep in the den? To my surprise, he went into the bedroom and closed the door…and to my surprise he stayed there until the next morning.

The Freedom of Forgiveness

I laid in my bed, but sleep was not on the agenda for me. My mind was racing, trying to make sense of it all. I wanted to know exactly what happened. I needed more details. I felt as if there was so much I did not know. I also wondered what would be next. Jeff had turned himself in—now what? I had never had any interaction with law enforcement or the judicial system, so I was completely lost.

I looked at the clock on my nightstand and it was after 3 a.m. "I need to find out from the detective what happens next," I thought to myself. But I dared not call him so in the early morning, not to mention it was now officially Christmas and the detective was definitely asleep and would be enjoying his family on Christmas Day. It's funny how in one house there can be gladness and joy celebrating the most wonderful time of the year, but in another house, in my house to be exact, there was only sadness and grief.

I couldn't wait for the day after Christmas. I had never in my life wanted so much to see the end of Christmas. There would certainly be no sleep for me, so for the rest of the night until the sun came up, all I could think about was, what's next? And just like that it was Christmas day.

As my oldest brother and stepfather started to move around in the house Christmas morning, I think we all had the same idea and feeling that we needed to get out of the house. So, one by one, we each said to the other, "I'll be back; I'm going to

The Freedom of Forgiveness

head out for a while." When I left the house, I went directly to my girlfriend Rhonda's house. Up until this time I had avoided communicating with her, even though she had made several attempts to contact me after she saw the story of my mother being murdered. It wasn't anything against her personally, I just didn't want to speak with anyone at that time, not even her. I had known her since middle school and we later became high school sweethearts, and I was extremely close to her family, and she became close to my mom. I knew that they would be celebrating and eating, so I felt as if I needed to be around some joy and fun. So off to her house I went. When I pulled into their driveway, I said to myself, "I hope they don't start asking me how I am doing and feeling. I hope they don't make me the center of attention." I got myself together and I walked up to their door and knocked. Her mom answered the door with the biggest smile on her face and immediately gave me a big hug. "Come on in," she said with joy and excitement. I walked into the house and all of her family embraced me with hugs, but they all had tears in their eyes. I didn't want to cry anymore, and I really didn't think I could, but sure enough, after a few hugs, tears began to roll uncontrollably down my face again.

Wait, I didn't come here for this. I didn't want to cry. So, I started telling them I was OK, and everything would be fine. Where was I getting this strength from? How was I holding it together? I know without a shadow of a doubt, it was because of my faith in God. A couple of years before my mother's death, I had accepted Jesus Christ as my personal Lord and Savior, and I had been attending church consistently. I wasn't a holy roller as they say, but I truly believed in God, and I was building my relationship with Him. And even though I was holding up pretty well, I had so many questions for God! I didn't blame God, but I questioned God.

After everyone had greeted me and we all had cried, it took a few moments for things to shift into a festive mode, but eventually they did. I tried to enjoy the moment, but I couldn't. My mind was beginning to be completely overwhelmed with anger, hate and revenge. In the midst of the fun, the music, the food and amazing people, all I could think about was making my younger brother pay for what he had done.

I finally decided to leave, and I told Rhonda that we would talk later. I left their house and I drove around for a few hours, wondering and pondering what role I could play in making sure that my younger brother would get the death penalty, or at least spend the rest of his life in prison. When I finally returned home, only my stepfather was there. Another harsh reality had set in: we had to plan a funeral. I told him not to worry, I would take care of everything, and I did. The day before my mother's funeral, the detective called to tell me that Jeff was petitioning the judge to allow him to attend.

"Over my dead body," I said. "I'll kill him if he sets one foot in that church."

And just like that, I was overwhelmed with anger and hate all over again. And at that point my mind became totally consumed with anger towards Jeff. The anger that I carried around for years was a cover up for my pain. If you hate a person, then you're defeated by them. Anger doesn't solve anything, but it can destroy everything. The anger of a person does not produce anything good.

"WHERE THERE IS ANGER, THERE IS PAIN"

It was now time to lay my mother to rest, and as the day of the funeral came, I constantly heard my mother's voice, telling me that day when I left for my doctor's appointment,

"I'm tired, I'm going to lay down and get some rest." Well, this was it, the day that we would lay her remains to rest.

My mother was truly my hero and role model. She was strong and courageous. She wasn't afraid of anything or anyone. She didn't have any education because she had to drop out of school in the 3rd grade to pick cotton in Georgia and take care of her younger siblings. She never had a childhood. She never had a father to love and lead her, so I felt like

The Freedom of Forgiveness

she spent a lot of her life looking for love in all the wrong men that would beat and abuse her. She met my father who was 25 years old when she was only 16 years old and got married and had her first child. By the time she was 20 years old she had 3 baby boys. When I was 3 years old my father left for work one day and never returned. He just walked out on us. He never gave any reason for leaving us and it would be years later that I would formally meet him. I learned how to persevere from my mother. She taught me to be strong and never give up. I grew up watching her work her fingers to the bone to keep a roof over our heads, put food on the table and clothes on our backs. Even though we didn't have much, my mom made the most of whatever we had. And so, on that day when she said she was going to lay down and get some rest, I now realized that perhaps her statement was symbolic. Even though she died a horrible and unthinkable death, I would later have some peace about the fact that she was finally resting from such a challenging and unfair life.

On the day of the funeral, I decided to reveal to many people in my family and friends something none of them probably knew, and that was the fact that I wrote poetry. I had written a special poem for my mom. It was my way of saying my final goodbye to the woman that I loved more than anyone in the world. The poem was titled, "I Used to Wonder."

When I was a child, I used to wonder who was this woman that cared.

The Freedom of Forgiveness

Why was it that she always shared?

I used to wonder where did the shoes come from that I had on my feet?

I used to wonder how did I get the food I always had to eat?

I used to wonder why did this woman always provide?

I used to wonder why regardless of what, she was always by my side.

I used to wonder why sometimes she would scream and shout.

I used to wonder why she would give to us and go without.

Now that I'm older and I'm finished with mischief and fun,

I realize she did all those things because she was our mom.

I know she was my angel sent from heaven up above,

The Freedom of Forgiveness

And now I don't wonder because

I know that was my mother's love.

Your love flowed like rivers of the Nile.

You will always be my mom,

And I will always be your child.

Looking back now after all these years, I realize that this poem didn't capture half of what my mother really meant to me, but it was written over twenty years ago. After the funeral the time came to head to the cemetery and bury my mother. I wasn't ready for this. It would truly be my last good-bye. As the funeral home limousine drove into the gates of the cemetery, reality started to set in - this was it, my mom was really gone, never to come back again. As we approached the area where she would be laid to rest, I tried to restrain myself from crying, but I couldn't. This was it. The car came to a stop and within seconds, my door was opened by one of the employees of the funeral home. I emerged directly in front of the hearse which had transported my mom's casket. My stepfather, my older brother and I went immediately to the hearse, along with a couple of my uncles, so that we could carry the casket to the grave. As we grabbed the casket, a silence overwhelmed me. I could see people walking and talking but I couldn't hear them. I could see the tree branches blowing, but I couldn't hear them. Other cars drove up and parked, but I couldn't hear them. As we carried the casket to the grave, it was as if everything and everyone was moving in slow motion. Suddenly, we stopped walking, and the silence was broken by one of the cemetery employees, telling us how to lay the casket down on the belts that would lower it in the ground.

The pastor finished speaking. "Ashes to ashes and dust to dust." We were told to lay our flowers on the casket, and the funeral home employee said, "This concludes the service." I walked over and dropped my flowers and said my final good-bye. And just like that, it hit me again, my mother was really gone. Glo was gone, never to return. I would never see her again in this life. The woman I knew all my life. The woman that taught me so many things. The woman that demonstrated perseverance and strength. The woman that loved me more than anyone ever would. The woman that was my hero. The woman that raised us the best she knew how, was gone. It was incredibly hard to grasp knowing this was it. I just couldn't wrap my mind around this new reality.

Chapter 4

Time For Justice

As I walked back to the car, I wasn't even off the grass where my mom had just been laid to rest before my rage and anger rose up. As much as I didn't want to leave my mom behind in this cemetery, I was even more determined to make sure that justice would be served. My brother had to pay for what he did. Before I reached the car, my tears had stopped, and I was no longer sad. Anger had taken the place of my sorrow and my only desire was to make my younger brother pay. On the way back to the church, all I could think about was getting justice and making sure that my younger brother paid for his crime.

I started thinking about the law and how I could make sure my younger brother would be prosecuted to the full extent of the law. I had no love or mercy for him in my heart. All I had in my heart for him was hate! This was now my life's mission. Nothing else seemed to matter - not my day job and not even my business. I would take the time off from both to accomplish my goal – and that was making sure that Jeff paid! I wanted him to suffer for the rest of his life.

The Freedom of Forgiveness

As we arrived back to the church and pulled into the parking lot, my thoughts were interrupted by the car driving over the speed bump in the parking lot. I had spaced out to the point that I didn't even realize that we were back at the church until we hit that speed bump.

What a day. It seemed so long but only a couple of hours had gone by between the actual funeral and the burial. As we all exited the limousines, people all headed to their cars. As for me, my oldest brother and my stepfather, we had all driven separately. I think we all drove separately because we all needed the space and time to process in our own way the finality of losing Glo forever. I don't think my oldest brother, or my stepfather went straight home after the funeral. I know I didn't. I just drove around for a couple of hours. I drove by the beach and parked there for a while. I just sat in my car watching the waves come in from the street.

The waves were loud and thunderous for some reason. They were interrupting my thinking, so I left and drove to a nearby park. As I sat in my car at the park my mind was flooded with so many thoughts and emotions. As I tried to process what I was thinking and feeling, it hit, I needed to get away. I needed to go somewhere and try to figure out what to do with all these thoughts of anger and hate for my younger brother. "That's it, I'm going to go somewhere," I thought to myself. So, I started the car and drove directly home. When I got home my stepfather and my oldest brother were there. When I walked in the house, I saw my stepfather laid out on the sofa in the den sleeping. And as I walked to my room my oldest brother's room door was closed. I stood in front of his door for a few seconds, and I could hear him snoring, so I figured he was sleeping also. It had been a long day and now that my mother was in her final resting place my mind shifted to "what was I going to do? How do I work to ensure that my younger brother pays for what he had done?" I laid down on my bed still wearing my suit from the funeral. I needed to figure some things out, so I decided to take a trip.

I didn't know where, but I knew I needed to go somewhere. As I thought about where to go my mind fell on the islands. I needed to go to the Caribbean islands. I didn't know exactly where, and I didn't care. I just knew I had to go. So, the next morning I called a travel agency and booked a trip to several Caribbean islands. Thankfully, I had some savings which is what I used to pay for my trip.

My mom's funeral had been covered by the proceeds from her life insurance policy and there was actually money designated from her insurance policy to my stepfather, my oldest brother and even my youngest brother. But due to what my youngest brother had done, the insurance company removed him as a beneficiary and split his portion between me, my stepfather and my oldest brother.

The Freedom of Forgiveness

It was 2 days after my mother's funeral, and I was on a plane to take some time to figure out what was next. No one knew where I had gone; I didn't tell my girlfriend, my stepfather, or my older brother. I know my decision to leave at this time may have seemed weird to them all, but it was what I needed to do at the time. I was being totally controlled by hate and anger, so I was not thinking rationally. I just left, and I was gone for a little over a week.

As I island-hopped, I found myself in Antigua, Guadeloupe and St. Croix. I experienced different thoughts and emotions on different islands. In Antigua I experienced some calmness. I think my experience in Antigua was the result of the fact that there weren't a lot of tourists there. It was a small quaint island, and the people were calm and extremely laid back. I stayed in Antigua for a couple of days.

As beautiful as this place was, I still found myself feeling sad and heart broken. I made it a point to go by the beach at night to just sit by the water and listen to the waves at night. As I would sit and listen to the waves, tears would begin to roll down my cheeks and all I could think about was my mother. I would cry out and even scream when I was flooded by my emotions. I would think about how I could have prevented everything and kept my mom alive. I wish I could have been at the house that day to defend and protect her. But all I could think about, was why did my younger brother murder our mother? I just wanted that one question answered. I would

The Freedom of Forgiveness

sit by the beach for hours and then make my way back to my hotel room a couple of hours before the sun began to rise. The days were okay, but my nights were filled with sadness. My time in Antigua came to an end, I was off to the next Island.

When I landed in Guadeloupe things were a little different there. There were more tourists, and the pace was just a little busier than Antigua. Guadeloupe was beautiful. The colorful buildings and crystal blue water beaches were like pictures on a postcard. I spent about 3 days on the island of Guadeloupe and those were actually good days. I went sightseeing in the daytime and I enjoyed the music and small cafes with live music as well. But just like in Antigua, at night I would go sit by the beach to listen to the waves roll in and out and cry and scream. I didn't see anything or anyone ever taking this deep sadness away.

Even though I was still sad, Guadeloupe actually took my mind off the anger that I was dealing with. It was therapeutic to feel some degree of normality even if only in small increments. I still had some sad moments in Guadeloupe, but it wasn't as bad as it was in Antigua. I still cried and screamed by the beach and thought about my mom. I didn't know what I wanted to accomplish by getting away. And as I island hopped, I was still unsure of what to do next in life. Finally, I was off to St Croix which would be my last island.

The Freedom of Forgiveness

I didn't think I was as sad anymore. Or at least I didn't think I would be crying and screaming anymore. Whatever island I found myself on, nothing could take away the hurt and pain and I would still find myself by the beach at night crying out to God and screaming and shouting. My emotions were mixed. I was angry at God, but then for some reason I would think to myself, "God must have a reason for this." Mind you, I didn't grow up in the church, nor was I a very strong Christian at this point, but for some strange reason I had faith that there was truly a purpose for why this happened. Of course, twenty-something years later, I now know, trust and believe that "all things work together for good to those who love God and are called according to His purpose." And part of that purpose is that I would later use my personal experiences to help others, and I would be able to tell them that no matter how bad something seems when it happens to you, God has a purpose and plan for allowing it to happen.

So, my faith in God caused me to have hope, but my grief caused me to feel anger and rage. One night, I went through my usual routine, eating dinner at the hotel around 7p.m. and then walking to the beach just after the sun had gone down. On this particular night, I did my usual--I cried, I screamed, and this night I yelled out to God.

I yelled out, "Why my Mama? Oh God why my Mama? Please God talk to me." I even cried out,

The Freedom of Forgiveness

"Bring her back God, I need my Mama. Please God, I need my Mama."

I couldn't stop crying for my Mama on this particular night for some reason. I don't know how loud I was crying out and I didn't even care. I was down a ways from my hotel and sitting at the edge of the water. I had thoughts of suicide in the sense that I didn't want to live without my mom. Life seemed so worthless. What did I have to live for?

But on this night, something was different. As I lay on the sand crying and sobbing, suddenly, the sky turned dark. Everything turned so black that I couldn't see my hands in front of my eyes. My sadness now turned to fear. I was so afraid that I laid down with my face covered with my hands in the sand. I didn't know if I was dreaming or imagining what was happening, but one thing I did know for sure, I was terrified out of my mind. As I lay with my face covered, I felt so afraid, shaking and praying for whatever was happening to stop, and all of a sudden, I heard a voice. An actual audible voice. The voice was loud but very calming at the same time, if that makes sense. And for some reason I couldn't determine which direction the voice was coming from. The voice just seemed to be surrounding me. It seemed to be coming from every direction. It was as if everything was at a standstill. The wind wasn't blowing, the waves were no longer moving, and it wasn't cold, hot or even warm - it just was. By this time, I really thought I must be dreaming. I thought about trying to peek to see where this voice was coming from, but I was too afraid. I had never experienced anything like this in my life. I felt as if I was the only one in the world at that moment. It was as if no other human beings existed. So, I laid there, and I listened. Who was this? And what did they want with me? I had so many thoughts running through my mind. But suddenly, a peace came all over me. A calmness arrested me. I suddenly felt safe and unafraid. The fear disappeared and peace replaced it. And as this peace and calmness came over my entire body, mind and spirit, I realized that God was speaking to me. I can honestly say without a doubt, that it was God's voice that I was hearing. God, the Almighty was speaking to me! Now I had never heard the audible voice of God before in my entire life, but everything within me knew that this was the voice of God. I had heard people say that His voice was reassuring and loving and that is exactly what I was hearing.

And because I finally realized that this was the voice of God, I removed my hands from covering my face and I sat up. It was still pitch dark and I still couldn't see anything or anyone, but I knew that the creator of the heavens and the earth was speaking to me. God was speaking to me. Suddenly, I broke out in tears. But this time my tears were not tears of sadness, they were tears of joy. I felt so loved and so cared for in that moment and I was listening intently to what God was saying to me. As I listened to His voice, God was telling me that He wanted me to go back home and tell others about His love and how much He cares for them. As He continued to talk to me, I realized that He had heard my prayers when I cried out to Him asking, "Why? Why my Mama? Why God?" is what I would always cry out. And now I was finally hearing why. God said, "I allowed you to hurt so that you could help others heal." He told me that my pain had purpose. He said that "I'm going to use you to show others how to forgive." At the time I didn't understand the fullness of what God was saying to me, but as He was speaking all I could do was cry and say, "OK God." And this book is the manifestation of what God said to me that night.

Remember, I did not grow up in church. I had only visited church when I was a little boy with a friend of mine who spent the summers in Florida. Although I had given my life to Christ a couple of years before my mom's murder, I wasn't a devout Christian. So, this was strange and confusing to me to say the least.

After His voice stopped, the deep darkness went away. I could hear the ocean waves again, and the fear that had gripped me had dissipated. I stood to my feet in total awe of what I had just heard and experienced. A part of me was thinking it was all a dream, but in my heart, mind and soul I knew that I had truly been in the presence of the spirit of God and truly heard His voice. I thought to myself this is why I had to leave home. It was starting to make some sense to me as I replayed everything that I had experienced. And suddenly, the light came on. I had this urgent feeling gripping my body and I just knew that whatever it was that God wanted me to do, I needed to go back home immediately and do it. I left the beach that night knowing that it was time for me to go back home.

So, I concluded my island-hopping, rearranged my plane tickets, and was back home a couple of days later. As I traveled back home that day, I knew that I needed to talk with my pastor. I knew that he would give me the advice I needed to guide me in the right direction. So, I sat back in peace for once and enjoyed the plane ride. Once I arrived home and settled in, I called my pastor to set up an appointment. When I called him, I had so much excitement that when he answered the phone, I just loudly yelled his name. "Pastor Johnson, Pastor Johnson. Oh my God!" I said. "You will never believe what happened to me." Before I could proceed telling him he told me to calm down and take a deep breath. And so, I did just that. He asked me if I was OK and I told him, "Absolutely Sir."

"What's going on? What's all the excitement about?"

I began to tell him what happened. I talked with him about my experience and the voice I heard, and what the voice had said. He didn't say anything while I was talking, just an "OK" from time to time. After I was finished sharing my experience with him, he said that he truly believed that I had heard the voice of God. The first thing he said to me was that God was calling me into the preaching ministry. I stopped and asked, "Calling me to preach? You mean I'm going to be a preacher? No way, are you serious?" I knew what God had told me, but I didn't know exactly how I was supposed to accomplish what God told me to do. My pastor could hear the fear and reservation in my voice and he asked, "Are you sure it was God talking to you?"

"Yes Sir."

He said, "Are you sure about what He told you to do?"

"Yes Sir."

He said, "Let me share something with you." He then began telling me about his own call, and he shared with me how it had been similar to what happened to me in terms of hearing God's voice. Not that he had lost his mom, but that he had heard the voice of God in the same manner. He then started sharing biblical stories of people who God called in an audible voice to do specific things. I was listening intently. He told me that the people in the bible days were no different from him and I. He said that people of today think that the people in the bible days were so super spiritual and godly that there's no way anyone in our day and time could match them, but he assured me that they were just regular people like us.

The Freedom of Forgiveness

He said he was convinced that I had heard the voice of God and that he was committed to helping me carry out whatever it was that God wanted me to do.

As I listened to him, I was comforted knowing that he understood and that he would be there for me. I didn't really know my dad growing up and he died when I was around twelve or thirteen years old. To have my pastor, a male figure, someone that I admired and respected tell me that he would be there for me made me feel like I could actually carry out what God told me to do. He then said to me that he knew this was a lot for me to take in and process and that he would be praying for me. He began to pray for me and as he started praying, I could feel the presence of God all over me again and joy began to overflood my soul.

After he finished praying with me, he said that he would be waiting for me to tell him when I was ready to do my first sermon. He also said that he wanted to recommend some books for me to read to help me with my first sermon preparation. "This was it," I started thinking to myself. I got quiet for a second and my pastor said these words, "God would never choose you if He couldn't use you." When he said these words to me, I knew that there was no turning back. I would hold on to these very words for the rest of my life. If God couldn't use me, He wouldn't have chosen me, wow! As the call came to an end, I actually had more questions than before, but I just figured that they would all be answered in time. But wow, ME, preach? There just seemed to be so much that I didn't know. I thought to myself, "Can I really do this?"

Eventually we met in person, and my pastor began to guide me and direct me in the things that I needed to do to prepare for what the Baptist church calls a "trial sermon." This is a sermon preached in front of the entire congregation, to be judged by them and the pastor. As he prepared me, the date came quickly for my trial sermon. I remember it as if it was yesterday. It was August 17, 1994, eight months after my mother was murdered. It was one of the most nerve-wrecking, but yet life-changing events of my life.

As I prepared over the weeks and months, I always thought about things like what if I can't do this? What if I fail? What if the voice I heard wasn't God? The doubt was overwhelming at times and when I would share my doubt with my pastor, he would always tell me that it's not about what you can do, but it's about what God wants to do through you. And so, I had to learn and understand that it wasn't about me, but it was all about God. I studied and I came up with a specific passage of scripture that really stuck out to me. I shared the passage of scripture with my pastor, and he started to quiz me to make sure I understood the passage of scripture. After several conversations and quizzing, I started to feel some level of confidence that I was ready. As I continued preparing it hit me one day. I thought that

The Freedom of Forgiveness

even when the worst thing that could ever happen to you happens, I realized that no matter how bad it was, some good could come out of it. I was feeling like everything was going to be alright. I did my trial sermon on my scheduled date as planned and after I finished, I became a licensed minister. What a life-changing event for me!

Shortly after my trial sermon, I became very involved with the youth ministry. I was also assisting the pastor wherever I was needed, but my passion was for the youth. Things were seemingly going OK. The pain and hurt of losing my mother had not gone away, but this new chapter in my life was giving me the strength I needed to live and move on, so I dove in with everything I had. Not only did I get involved heavily with my church, I also got involved in the community that I had grown up in.

Collier City was your typical urban, low-income, under-served and impoverished hood-like area. The street corners were home to school dropouts as well as prostitutes, drug dealers, and any other criminal element that existed. Collier City had a reputation throughout South Florida. It was a part of the City of Pompano Beach, but jokingly, some claimed it was its own country. I had been blessed to make it out without selling drugs, getting arrested or killed, so I decided to give back, to try to make a difference in the lives of the youth and other people in my old neighborhood. I started a non-profit organization, and I named it the P.I.P. Group which stood for Power In the People.

The Freedom of Forgiveness

My co-founder was my girlfriend, Rhonda, who also grew up in Collier City. She and I managed to convince about five of our old neighborhood friends to be a part of the organization as well. This was meaningful and fulfilling for me and helped keep my mind sane to a degree. Our organization would go on to do mentoring for the troubled youth in Collier City, job fairs, and neighborhood trash clean-ups, where we worked out a partnership with Home Depot, a home improvement store that donated supplies such as industrial plastic bags, gloves and rakes. We also assisted the elderly in my old neighborhood by removing old bulk trash and furniture from their yards and inside their homes. We also painted the homes of the elderly with paint donated to us by Home Depot.

Despite the trauma and tragedy, I thought I was moving on with my life and not allowing my rage, anger, hurt and "unforgiveness" to control me. As a result of the community work that my organization was doing, I was later offered employment by the local police department as a community specialist/liaison. It was a no-brainer. I didn't have my mom as my business partner in the cleaning business anymore, so I didn't want to carry on with that. I would much rather work for the police department than continue my job at the warehouse. So, I closed the business, resigned from the warehouse, and began my career with the police department. It really seemed as if I had totally moved on with my life and had left behind the hate, bitterness, hurt, anger and unforgiveness for my younger brother.

The Freedom of Forgiveness

As an employee of the police department, I helped eradicate drug dealers out of my old neighborhood by doing anti- drug rallies and getting residents out to partner with the police in getting rid of the drug dealers. We used an initiative called the Wrice Process, and I was trained by the late Mr. Herman Wrice, of Philadelphia. We held rallies and protests with the slogan, "Up with hope, down with dope," on certain weekdays and every weekend.

The initiative became so popular that I began to train residents and different police agencies in the South Florida tri-county area, and even traveled to different states training other residents and police departments in the Wrice Process. Life was busy for me. I kept myself busy as I did ministry work as the youth director and worked for the local police department. I purposely kept myself as busy as I could because it helped me not to think about what my younger brother had done. But no matter how busy I kept myself, whenever things slowed down or I had a break, the unforgiveness, anger, and hurt would creep back in and most times overwhelm me.

When these feelings came back all I could think about was that he would have to pay for what he had done, and I would make sure that he did. As my life was moving on, so was the process of trying and convicting Jeff of first-degree murder. I was the point of contact for the family in dealing with the state attorney's office. My personal goal was to make sure that my younger brother would get the worst available penalty, the death penalty. I attended all the hearings and court proceedings, alone for the most part. Every now and then my aunt would attend, but I was at every hearing and communicated closely with the state prosecutor.

    I emphatically made it clear that I would settle for nothing less than life in prison for my younger brother, but I told the prosecutor to push for the death penalty. I was not familiar with the court proceedings and the process of a trial at the time. All I knew is that I wanted justice at any and all cost. As the proceedings started, my younger brother was afforded a public defender lawyer for his defense. I was disgusted that anyone would defend someone who murdered their mother in cold blood. My anger went to a whole new level, and I was determined all the more to get justice. As the system goes, the public defender asked if we wanted to do a plea bargain. If not, the defense would be temporary insanity, and the public defender was sure Jeff would not get life in prison or the electric chair. Driven by rage and hate, I would have no part of a plea bargain. I no longer saw him as my brother; I saw him as a cold-blooded killer. I was determined to see that justice prevailed, if it was the last thing I did in life.

"UNFORGIVENESS WILL EMPOWER THOSE WHO OWE YOU TO OWN YOU"

The Freedom of Forgiveness

During the process of preparing for the trial, the state prosecutor and I became pretty good friends, to the extent that he would not only discuss the trial with me, but we would also discuss personal matters. I remember him talking to me about his kids, what sports they were involved in, their grades, and their overall family life. He was driven by his responsibility to an oath he took, and I was driven by anger, hate and unforgiveness. Months went by, and still no trial. I learned all about continuances and being trial ready. I practically lived at the courthouse. I was at the courthouse so much that I learned the names of courtroom clerks and deputies, and some of the staff of the state attorney's office. The prosecutor would call me and say, "Mr. Jackson, it's shaping up and looking good."

Then on that day he finally said, "Mr. Jackson, we're ready to proceed with the trial."

I was more than ready; it had been months and months, and I was tired of all of the stalling by the public defender's office. Knowing that the state prosecutor would not make a move or decision without first consulting me, I was able to continue to do ministry and police work without the fear of my younger brother finding some kind of loophole. It was almost time; all of the stalling tactics and attempts to use temporary insanity as a defense was coming to a close. I remember being in the courtroom during all the hearings and hating to see my younger brother as he was brought into the courtroom in his jail jumpsuit, ankle cuffed as well as handcuffed. Whenever I could stomach looking at him, all I wanted to do was run over and choke him to death. My life was being consumed by hate, anger and revenge, but I was still active in ministry and work in between dealing with those emotions. But honestly, the priority was revenge which was driven by rage.

One day, while I was at my office working, I received a call from the state prosecutor telling me that the judge had finally set a trial date. "Wow, finally!" I was ecstatic. By this time, it had been months since Jeff had murdered our mother, but finally, all of the stalling was over. I was way past ready to get justice for our mom. Rage, hate and anger was always driving me, and I really didn't care what my other family members wanted, all that mattered at this time is what I wanted, and what I was trying to accomplish. I was just charging ahead with one goal in mind and that goal was to make sure that justice was served and that my younger brother would spend the rest of his life in prison or die in the electric chair. He needed to pay for what he did, and I would not stop until he got what he deserved, which in my opinion was the death penalty or life in prison.

Chapter 5

Where Do I Go From Here?

A week before the trial was to start, I was more than ready. As I look back, I realize now that I didn't have a life. I was like a zombie. I was consumed and controlled by anger, hate and unforgiveness. My younger brother was in shackles, handcuffs and a jail cell, but I too was locked up—not with chains or in a jail cell but imprisoned by unforgiveness. My freedom had been taken away, and I didn't even realize it. All I knew is that I would never forgive Jeff, and I never wanted to see his face again after the trial.

"UNFORGIVENESS IS A PRISON, BUT FORGIVENESS IS THE KEY THAT UNLOCKS THE PRISON DOORS AND SETS YOU FREE"

Despite my obsession for justice, things were going pretty well with my job at the police department and even better in the ministry. The youth department had grown, and as the youth director,

The Freedom of Forgiveness

I was doing really cool youth events and building great relationships with the youth in the church. I had also become one of the favorite ministers in the church— so much so, that whenever the senior pastor went out of town, the congregation would request that I preach. We had at least seven or eight other ministers at the time, but I was a favorite, probably because I preached similarly to our senior pastor. Not only were opportunities available for me at our church, but opportunities started opening up for me to preach at other churches around the city. I was embracing it all because it kept me busy, and I was able to function in spite of losing my mother. From the outside looking in, it appeared as though I had it all together and it seemed as if my life had taken a turn for the better even though my world had been turned completely upside down when my mother was murdered.

The fact of the matter is that I was dying on the inside from the cancerous disease of unforgiveness. It was so ironic that I was a licensed minister, and I was preaching all around town the message of hope, unconditional love, and forgiveness, yet I was hell-bent on justice, revenge, and the death of my brother. I had pity, love and concern for so many people, but none for my own brother. All I had for him was rage, hate, anger and unforgiveness.

And so, as the trial date approached, I found myself dealing with all kinds of conflicting emotions and feelings. It was a roller coaster ride for me. As I was maturing as a Christian and a licensed minister, I was also battling with my thoughts of revenge and justice. Leading up to the start of the trial, I would have days where I was one hundred percent ready and sure that my younger brother deserved the death penalty or life in prison. But some days I would be in conflict with myself, wondering if I was doing the right thing.

Almost fourteen months had passed, and it was time for justice. The state prosecutor was ready and confident that we would get the death penalty or life in prison. That had been my goal from the beginning. However, in the days leading up to the trial, something was going on inside of my head and my heart. I felt confused, and I started doubting myself.

"Was I doing the right thing?" I started thinking.

I didn't communicate any of my feelings and emotions to the state prosecutor because I didn't want him to know what I was dealing with. I needed him to stay focused on the goal, since it was becoming confusing for me to do so. So as the start of the trial came closer, every time I spoke with the state prosecutor, I continued in the vein that I had started in, demanding justice for my mom.

It was finally here, the first day of the trial. I remember waking up that morning and experiencing that same feeling I experienced at my mother's burial, the feeling of everything being and moving in slow motion. I was lethargic and robotic, and my mind was filled with a plethora of racing thoughts. As I brushed my teeth, it was as if I was in a sci-fi movie, just weird and inexplicable. As I shaved and showered, everything was heightened. The sound of the water was as loud as the sound of a waterfall. The lights in the bathroom were extremely bright and strangely warmer than normal and seemed to beam directly and specifically in my face. This was the day that I had fought so hard to see, and it was nothing like I thought it would be.

I struggled to get dressed and gather my thoughts and myself together in order to make it to the courthouse on time. After all, it was the first day of trial. I needed to be on time and in my mode of hate, anger and revenge as I sat in the courtroom. It seemed as if it took days to shower, shave, brush my teeth and get dressed in my best suit.

Finally, I was ready. I got into my car. I put the key into the ignition. As the engine turned over, I seemed to hear each individual sound involved in the process of starting the car. As I gripped the steering wheel tightly, I could literally feel anger, hate and rage all through my arms and wrist. My entire body started to get tense and tight. I wasn't clear about what was happening to my body, but it didn't feel good. I didn't like this feeling and I honestly didn't want to feel what I was feeling. This was the first time that I was starting to realize how my hatred and rage for my younger brother was affecting me physically. It was as if I had no control over my body and I had no choice but to feel what I was feeling. As I started to back my car up, I turned on the radio hoping that would help me shake what I was feeling, but it didn't. It was as if the music intensified what my body was feeling, but no matter what, I needed to get to the courthouse. I pulled off slowly and I was finally on my way. I decided to roll my windows down hoping that the fresh air blowing through my car would help me with the way I was feeling.

I made my way to I-95 heading south downtown to the courthouse. Even though my radio was on, and there was a little engine noise along with the noise of the wind, suddenly my car became completely quiet. It was as if I was in a capsule or some sort of tunnel. And just like that dark night on the beach 14 months ago, again I clearly heard the voice of God. And just as it did then, His voice would change the direction of my life for the rest of my life.

"Look at you," God said to me calmly, but with conviction. He was reasoning with me. He was talking to me as if we were riding in the car together. Unlike at the beach when His voice was thunderous and loud, he was simply conversing with me. I began to speak back to God.

"What do you mean, look at me?" I was confused and so I asked again, "What do you mean?"

The Freedom of Forgiveness

God answered. "Aren't you a minister of the Gospel of grace? Don't you preach love and forgiveness? So, what are you doing? Where is the grace and forgiveness for your own brother? Where is the love for your own brother?"

I replied angrily, "But God—he killed my mother! He needs to pay. He needs to suffer for what he did! I'm getting justice for my mother, that's what I'm doing."

If someone passing by me would have looked into my car, they would have thought I was crazy because it seemed as if I was talking to myself. Of course, this was before Bluetooth in cars. I continued to say, "He needs to suffer, he needs to suffer!" And then I said, "He needs to die."

My emotions were elevating to the point that I was screaming. "I hate him God, I hate him!" And as I continued to scream, I started sobbing. With tears rolling down my cheeks, I said, "Please God, make him pay. I just want him to pay God, I just want justice!" In agony, I cried out louder, "I just want justice God!"

"Justice? Who placed justice in your hands? Who are you to seek justice?"

"But God, he killed my mother! I will never get her back," I continued. "It's not fair God, it's just not fair."

As I continued to sob, I continued saying, "I just want justice. Please God, just give me justice."

But God said, "Justice is mine."

His voice was very soft, comforting and loving. As He continued to talk to me, my tears stopped, and calmness came all over me. There was a peace overtaking me that I had not felt in a long time. My heart, mind and emotions were now calm. For the first time I started to feel that everything was going to be okay. For the first time since losing my mother I felt that I would be fine and that my life would go on.

God told me that I was allowing hurt, anger, rage and revenge to poison my heart, and that it was not my job to seek justice, but it was my job to forgive and to show grace towards my brother. "OK, God," I asked with some confusion, "tell me, what am I supposed to do?"

God's answer was unequivocal. "Let this go. Let the system do what it's in place to do, and you walk away from this case and never look back."

"THE TOUGHEST THING ABOUT FORGIVENESS IS FORGIVING SOMEONE WHO HASN'T ASKED FOR FORGIVENESS"

By this time, I was looking for a parking space at

The Freedom of Forgiveness

the courthouse. When I found a space, I sat in my car for a few minutes. I needed to digest all that God had said to me. I had spent months being the point person and the family spokesperson to make sure that justice was served, and that Jeff paid for what he had done.

And now I was being told by God to walk away. Even though I was feeling peace and I knew I had to let this go, my brain was full of what ifs. What if they let him off easy? What if they find him insane and send him to some mental facility and then release him after just a few years? And how was I going to explain this to the state prosecutor? How was I going to explain the conversation I had with God to this man? Would he think I was crazy? I didn't even know if he was a Christian or if he even believed in God. What would he think, after all that I had demanded and fought for?

And then it was as if God whispered softly and said to me again, "Just walk away."

I gathered myself together and got out of my car and starting walking to the courthouse. As I walked, I was arrested by silence again. I could see people walking, laughing and talking but I couldn't hear them. I could see cars moving, but I could not hear them. As I reached the courthouse checkpoint, the silence broke and the everyday noise of people talking and footsteps echoing hit me like bricks. As I waited in a crowd for the elevator, I began to think about what God had told me to do. The elevator opened and me and all the people walked in. The elevator was moving fast, and the voices of those talking seemed extra loud. But in the midst of this chaotic moment, I started replaying my conversation with God. I didn't understand everything God had told me and why, but I knew I had to do what He told me to do. I stood in the elevator with all these people and suddenly it was as if I was the only one in the elevator. The voices stopped and I started to feel as light as a feather. I felt as if a ton of bricks had been lifted off my shoulders. Everything was gone - the rage, the anger, the tense feeling in my body and even the desire to make sure my younger brother would receive the death penalty or life in prison.

The elevator stopped and I stepped out. I immediately ran into the state prosecutor as he was standing right in front of the elevator. "It's time," he said. He was jubilant, smiling and ready, but all I could do for a few seconds was stare at him.

"Mr. Jackson, are you OK? What's wrong?"

"Yes, yes I'm just fine," I answered.

"Let's go; our courtroom is this way." He started to lead me to the courtroom.

"I need to talk to you before we go into the courtroom."

The Freedom of Forgiveness

He asked me again, this time with a deeper concern, "Are you sure you're OK, Mr. Jackson?"

"Is there somewhere we can talk in private," I asked him.

He led me to a small room furnished with a desk and two chairs. I sat down. He sat too, but reluctantly. "I know this is hard for you and I know it's very emotional for you," he said. "But it's time to get justice for your mother. We don't have long; the proceedings will start in about ten minutes."

I finally mustered up enough courage and strength to say, "I'm done."

"What do you mean, you're done?"

"I'm done with this case; I'm done with my brother. I'm done with everything."

I can still remember the look on his face— confused, perplexed, a somewhat angry look.

"What do you mean," he said as he raised his voice. "We've worked so hard to get justice for your mother!"

I replied again, "I'm done, I'm finished. Let the judge or the jurors do whatever they feel is right. I can't be a part of this trial anymore. It's time for

The Freedom of Forgiveness

me to let everything go and move on with my life," I told him. I stood up, looked directly into his eyes and I thanked him for everything. I then apologized to him for my change of heart, and I told him that I appreciated all that he had done. I put my hand out to shake his hand. At first, he didn't respond, but after a few seconds he shook my hand. I could feel his anger emanating from his body, but I knew I had to obey God. I couldn't worry about his anger. This wasn't about him; it was about me.

I turned to the door and walked out of that room, and I went straight to the elevator. As I waited for the elevator, I watched the prosecutor walk away. He turned toward the courtroom and entered it. The elevator opened and I walked in.

As the elevator descended, I began to feel a lightness and a release of pressure from all over my body. This feeling continued to overwhelm me. As I walked back to my car, things seemed different. I wasn't tense anymore. I didn't have anxiety anymore. I had a peace within me that I had not had since my mother was murdered. For the first time since then, I felt as if everything was going to be alright. I got in my car. A tiny smile came across my face, and I left that parking lot and I never looked back.

The next morning, I woke up as a different person in a different world. I could hear birds; they seemed to sing louder and more distinctly than before. I looked out the window and the sun seemed brighter. The sky was clear and blue. I didn't know what the future would hold, but I was ready to take it one day at a time.

I got a call from the state prosecutor a few days later. By this time, he had calmed down and he was polite and respectful, but I could still hear some level of resentment in his voice. The trial was over already, and he told me Jeff would be sentenced to seventeen years in state prison, with no possibility of parole. I really didn't care to hear any more of what he had to say, so I thanked him again. "God bless you," I told him. "Goodbye."

I sat down and it hit me: where do we go from here? And personally, where do I go from here? It was time for me to move on with my life. Later that day, I did call my stepfather and my older brother to tell them the outcome of the trial. To this day, I have never had any detailed or intimate conversation with them about their emotional/mental process and what they were experiencing. We never spoke about anything concerning how we were doing and coping. I kept them informed when I was involved in the trial and at times, I got a little angry at them because I felt as though they didn't care as much as I did. I would later realize that my obsession was only because I was being driven and controlled by unforgiveness.

The Freedom of Forgiveness

I learned that people process their grief and pain differently, and that the fact that they were not being driven and controlled by unforgiveness as I was did not mean they didn't hurt as much as I did.

Honestly, I felt numb after speaking with the state prosecutor. It was kind of surreal: had this really happened? Once again, I was reminded that my mother was really gone and the family I had known all my life was shattered and broken forever.

Chapter 6

The Letter

Unforgiveness is somewhat like cancer. It can lie dormant for years, but all it takes is a routine checkup — and just like that, your life can be changed forever. Cancer is a disease that eats away at your inside organs and ultimately causes the body to shut down and succumb, basically to a slow death. And so it is with unforgiveness. Unforgiveness will hide silently in our hearts and minds, but all the while it's eating away at us. This is another kind of slow death, not physical, but emotional, psychological and spiritual. Usually when cancer develops inside our bodies, we are unaware at the beginning.

Eventually, though, signs and symptoms begin to manifest. For some, the official diagnosis is made after a routine annual physical. For others, the symptoms may remain ignored or undetected for sustained periods of time. Then, after the diagnosis, we often try to hide the fact that the cancer exists, as if it's some self-inflicted disease that should cause us to be ashamed. I find the same to be true of unforgiveness.

At first it goes largely undetected. We may have suppressed or repressed feelings of anger, hate, or rage toward someone, but fail to make the connection between those symptoms, if you will, and the underlying disease of unforgiveness. Oftentimes, its not until some kind of check-up, in the form of a sermon, a billboard, a bumper sticker or perhaps even a confrontation with the individual who is the object of our unforgiveness, do we begin to even realize that the unforgiveness exists. And still yet, even at that point, some try to ignore the feeling, forget about it, hoping that one day it will just go away. But just like cancer, when left undetected, unaddressed, or left untreated it has the potential to cause extreme damage.

"IT'S TIME FOR YOU TO WALK IN FREEDOM"

My checkup was a letter. Life was moving right along for me. I had married my high school Sweetheart and I was working for the police department and traveling around the country, helping other communities fight drugs in their neighborhoods; and I was being used in ministry as a youth pastor in my local church. I was given opportunities to speak and minister to other churches as well. I was out preaching and teaching love, forgiveness and restoration, not realizing that what I was preaching, I still wasn't living. As one of the ministers, I assisted Pastor Johnson at funerals. It took me a while to be able to do that, because funerals were a constant reminder of my loss. They took me back to a place of hurt

The Freedom of Forgiveness

and grief around what my brother had done. When I finally felt ready to assist Pastor Johnson again, he welcomed me back and told me I could step away if it got hard for me again.

On this particular Saturday, I was assisting him with a funeral. As usual, I presided over the funeral service and would assist Pastor Johnson at the burial. It was a normal Saturday, nothing out of the ordinary, and certainly a normal funeral. After the service, we headed to the cemetery for the burial. Everything went well; the service at the church was seamless and the final burial at the cemetery also went smoothly. I felt basically okay, and so I was happy thinking that maybe this was it; maybe I was in the clear, away from the pain and grief and anger that had haunted me since the murder of my mother.

After the burial, Pastor Johnson and I rode back to the church together. There was some small talk between us, but nothing serious. As we pulled into the church parking lot, Pastor Johnson informed me that he had a letter addressed to me at the church. It had been in his office for a few days. So, after parking, instead of getting in my car and leaving, I followed him to his office and sat down. He went to the bathroom to change out of his robe, and as he was changing, he loudly said, "The letter is somewhere there on my desk addressed to you." I was flipping through a magazine when he came out of the bathroom, and he scrabbled through the papers on his desk. Finally, I heard him say, "Here it is, here's the letter."

The Freedom of Forgiveness

I took the letter and looked at the return address. It was from someone who's last name was Williams. I actually had no idea who it was. The next thing I noticed was that it was from a Florida correctional institution. Maybe, I thought, this was a kid from one of my youth mentorship programs. Maybe I had mentored him, and he still went in the wrong direction, ended up in prison, and was writing to me to touch bases. I didn't know, I had no idea. Although it was important to me to see who the letter was from, I didn't feel any sense of urgency about opening it. So, I put it in my jacket pocket, and as I reached my car and got inside, I folded my jacket and put it on the seat in my car and headed home. Getting home was about a twenty-minute drive, and in all that time it never occurred to me that I should at least skim through the letter whenever I stopped at a red light. I was focused on getting home and changing out of the hot black suit I was wearing from the funeral.

I finally reached home, I grabbed my suit jacket and was getting ready to open my car door, when I was struck with a desire to read the letter. I pulled the letter out of my jacket and looked at the name of the sender again. Still, I had no idea who this person was. I opened the letter, being careful not to rip away the sender's information. I began to read the letter, and I froze.

"Allen," the letter read, "I know you don't want anything to do with me, so I sent this letter with a fake name because I knew that if I would have put my name on the letter you would have just thrown it away."

At this point I realized that it was from my brother. This letter was from Jeff. My first thought was to stop reading it and to destroy it. "How had he found me?" I thought to myself. By this time, it had been a few years since he had been locked up in prison, and we had not communicated at all. How had he known to send it to the church I was attending? Who had he been talking to? Who had given him my church information and address?

Curiosity made me refocus and continue reading. As I continued reading the letter I was gripped with sadness. I started to weep. Jeff was explaining that he was diagnosed with schizophrenia and mental illness. He explained that he wasn't in his right mind when he murdered our mother. Over the years I lost the letter, but from what I remember, it basically was his acknowledgment of what he had done. He explained that he and our mother had gotten into a heated argument because she wouldn't give him money. The argument became a shoving match, and finally Mama told him to get out of her house. He went into the den and unlocked the back door; then he left out of the front door and went down the street. He waited until he figured she was asleep. His initial intention was to go into her room to steal money from her. When he came back to the house, he entered through the back door, which he had left unlocked earlier, and walked quietly through the house. He said he was still angry, so he went to his room and got a handgun he had and approached the door to her room which was closed. He listened outside of her door with the handgun in his hand by his side, and heard light snoring, so he turned the knob and entered. Her purse wasn't on the dresser where he expected it to be. He looked around the room, hoping to see her purse, but he didn't see it. And just as he started to leave her room, he recalled being really angry and then all of a sudden, he heard voices in his head, telling him to kill her. And out of all the days that he had come over to the house, on this day he had a gun. He said that the voices got louder and louder, to the point where he felt like his head was going to burst. He stood at the side of her bed, staring at her. The voices got louder and louder. "Do it, do it," the voices said. "Just do it and get it over with. She hates you anyway. She told you to get out. She doesn't want anything to do with you."

    He stood there, wanting the voices to stop, but also feeling as if the voices were right. He said it seemed as if he had been standing there with the gun in his hand forever. Before he knew it, he pointed the gun at her head. Seconds later, as he could no longer take hearing the voices, he pulled the trigger, and a loud bang stopped the voices. He had shot her in her head at point-blank range. After he realized what happened, the voices started back up again, telling him to wait for me and to kill me too when I came home to pick Mama up for work. So, he left her bedroom and waited to see if I would come.

The Freedom of Forgiveness

And I thought to myself, "Of all the days for me to look at buying a new car for the business, I chose that one." I didn't come home right away as I normally would have.

Then suddenly, the voices ceased, and it was as if he snapped out of a trance. He ran back into our mother's room, only to see blood on her face, pillows and the floor. At that moment, he panicked and ran into the room Kevin slept in and hid the gun under a dresser. Then he ran out the door. He kept running until he got tired and stopped at a phone booth to call a friend to pick him up.

The letter said how sorry he was and he asked me to forgive him. He told me that he was sick, and he didn't mean to hurt Mama. He said he needed help because he felt that he was crazy. As I continued to read the letter, he started talking about something interesting. He talked about our days as little boys and how he had felt abandoned by me because, as we got older, I never spent time with him and our family because I was always with my friends. He went on to say that when I left to go into the U.S. Army after high school that he really felt lost and abandoned. We were all we had, he said, and I had left the family.

"You left us," he wrote.

He told me again that he was sick and that's why he killed our mother. He said that I would probably never understand and that he wouldn't blame me if I never forgave him. He said that he was telling me these things, not to get me to feel sorry for him or pity him, but because he had gotten to a place in his life where he felt lost and alone. I found out later that he had in fact, been officially diagnosed with schizophrenia while in prison, and was in the mental health ward and on medication. I kept reading.

He continued telling me about his struggles as a young man and what led him into a life of homosexuality. It was as if he was pouring his life out right before me, walking me through his life as he had lived it. It's amazing how you can live in the same house and grow up together with your siblings and have no idea what's going on in their life. I never knew any of these things that he was sharing with me, and they were eye-opening, to say the least.

As he poured out his heart, it did not take away the fact that he had murdered our mother. It certainly didn't take away the pain and hurt I had experienced all these years. But at that moment, I realized that there's a reason why people do what they do. As horrible as it was that he had murdered our mother, as crazy as it was, and regardless of whether I accepted all that he had shared - this was his reason. It didn't make things better or OK, but it opened my eyes and most importantly my heart.

He continued pouring his life out before me. As I read, I began to look back on life and remember some of the things he wrote about, especially how he felt about our biological father never being there and how it impacted him. He talked about the times he and I would pretend that we were men and married with our families and we would imagine living next door to each other. I remembered those things; I remembered how we would have these little, tiny cars and build homes out of playing cards and pretend we were successful businessmen with perfect wives and kids. All we ever wanted was a family, a real family.

By the time I got to the end of the letter, I was crying uncontrollably, overwhelmed with emotions. I was sad; I was sympathetic. I felt guilty in some strange way, and I felt responsible to a degree for some of his difficulties in life. I knew that the way he turned out in life was because of the choices he made, but I thought that maybe his life would have turned out differently if our father had been in our lives and if we had had a "real family." A family with a strong, wise, supportive and loving father that loved our mother and provided for his family. One thing I know is that a real father, as I described, makes a major difference in the lives of his children. It doesn't guarantee perfect and successful children, but it does increase the chances of children growing up and becoming successful.

I would later find out from my stepfather that Jeff had written me at least fifty letters that were mailed to the house address, but I had moved out and gotten married. My stepfather told me that he had thrown them away because he didn't want my younger brother disturbing my life.

"You had already moved on. The past was the past."

I accepted that and I actually appreciated my stepfather's actions. Time really does heal and help with the worst of experiences. At the end of the letter, Jeff stated that he knew he had to do the time for the crime he committed. He said that every day in prison was a living hell for him. He said that most of his days were spent thinking about suicide or thinking that he wouldn't make it out of prison alive. He went on to describe prison life briefly, and truthfully, I thought he wouldn't make it out alive because he was a small man in stature. In closing, he told me that he would understand if I never responded to his letter and that he would never try to reach me again. He wrote "I'm sorry" and the words "PLEASE FORGIVE ME" in big letters and signed his name, Jeff.

I sat there in my car holding this letter while tears fell from my eyes and rolled down my cheeks. I had not had any communication with him for years, and now out of nowhere, he had come back into my life through this letter. I managed to get myself together enough to get out of the car and walk into the house. Rhonda greeted me, and I burst into tears all over again. I felt weak in my knees. I stumbled into the bedroom and lay on the bed, sobbing uncontrollably.

The Freedom of Forgiveness

"What's wrong baby? What's wrong? Rhonda asked as she began to weep.

I couldn't talk. I had so many emotions and thoughts overtaking me. My feelings ranged from feeling guilty to feeling extremely sad. I felt guilty because of how I had initially made it my number one priority to see Jeff die or spend his life in prison. At that moment, I felt so much regret for the anger, disgust and rage I had directed at Jeff. Until this letter arrived in my life, I didn't know any of these things that he had shared in his letter. At this stage in my life, if I had known these things, I don't think I would have harbored so much anger, rage and hate for Jeff. His letter was like a mirror. As I read it, I saw myself and my hate-filled heart that I had never realized how bad it was until now. I also felt sad. Sad because I knew that Jeff would not get the help he needed in prison.

Prison doesn't rehabilitate people. In my opinion, prisons either destroy you as a human being or they make you into something that you would spend years trying to overcome once you're released. Sad because I knew that he was in a living hell, not to mention the fact that he would have to live the rest of his life with what he had done. I also felt responsible to a degree for some of Jeff's experiences he mentioned in his letter, mainly because his letter revealed to me how important I was to our little family unit. We were all we had, and I left. I left immediately after high school and went into the Army. I was thinking,

"What if I had stayed home and helped him through what he was dealing with as a teenager" Maybe it was wishful thinking to feel as though I could have helped him, but my heart had been touched by his letter and I just felt like there was something I could have done. I just couldn't pull myself together and stop crying. Rhonda continued asking me what was wrong but I couldn't form any words. All I could do was weep and weep some more. This letter had really touched my heart. Compassion was birthed in me for my younger brother - compassion I had never felt for him before in my entire life. His letter wasn't going to bring our mother back and it didn't excuse him for what he had done, but it did touch my heart and caused me to feel something towards him I never thought I would ever feel for him, and that was compassion.

Chapter 7

The Journey to Forgiveness

I cried until I couldn't cry anymore. I had no tears left in me. When I finally got myself together somewhat, I started thinking "What was next? What should I do?" I had to write back to Jeff. But what would I say? I didn't know what to write. No wise words came to me. I just knew I had to respond. Finally, I took a sheet of paper out and just started writing. I started it out with, "I got your letter that you sent to my church." Then I wrote, "This is my home address, and this is my home phone number. You can call me collect."

There had been a time in my life when I decided that I no longer had a younger brother. Because of the hurt he had brought to our family and the pain that he caused me; I literally did not acknowledge him as my brother. There were conversations at work, at church when I was asked how many brothers and sisters I had. I would say, "I only have an older brother." I had erased my younger brother's existence. During that time, I would not have believed anyone could have told me that I would ever acknowledge him, let alone communicate with him again.

But now, I felt as if chains had fallen off me and shackles were released from my ankles and my wrists. I was free and I could feel it all over me. Looking within myself and coming to an understanding that Jeff had mental issues, I found the capacity and willingness to communicate with him and to eventually forgive him. I knew at that moment that I had that capacity only because of the love of God that had grown and matured inside of me, and I knew I had to forgive Jeff for me and not for him.

"FORGIVENESS ISN'T FOR OTHERS, IT'S FOR YOU, LETTING GO LETS YOU GO"

After this communication, I would later visit him in prison, and even support him financially at times by sending him money. *Martin Luther King said, "Only love can drive out hate and only light can drive out darkness."* I had allowed hate and darkness to fill my heart and control my emotions and my actions. In the end, I was in a dark prison, and I didn't even realize it.

Looking back, I can truly say that Jeff's letter caused me to realize what I had kept in my heart for years and how it had turned me into someone that wasn't truly me. That person that I had become was calm and loving on the surface, but full of hatred, anger and fury underneath. Strangely enough, as the days went by, I realized that I had to forgive my mother as well as Jeff. Yes, I had to forgive my mother, I was mad at her for dying. I was mad at her for not locking her door that day - because I thought that perhaps when he had tried to open her door, the noise would have awoken her, and maybe she would have had a chance to protect herself. This thought, while it was selfish and probably unrealistic, haunted me for years. I also had to forgive myself for not being there that day to protect her. Even as a little boy, not having our father in our lives, I always felt that I had to protect my mother. For years I blamed myself for not heading directly home after my doctor's appointment. Maybe I could have protected her and saved her. Jeff's letter had started me on a journey…a journey to freedom from the past.

Every day I would try to figure out what I was going to say when my brother called. Every day I would ponder possible conversations. Days passed, and I didn't hear back from him. All kind of thoughts began going through my mind. Had he killed himself, thinking that I wouldn't respond or hadn't gotten his letter? Maybe I had made a mistake giving him my personal contact information. After five or six days had gone by, my anticipation and anxiety had dwindled and fizzled out. I didn't know what to think.

The Freedom of Forgiveness

A week or so after I had written back to Jeff, I was back into my routine, working twelve to fourteen-hour days. This day, I finished work and I reached home around eight o'clock. I went straight to my chair to sit down and relax for a while. I called Rhonda over and we chatted for a few minutes. About two minutes later the phone rang, and I hauled myself out of my chair to answer it.

After I said, "Hello," the phone was silent for a minute and then an automated voice recording asked if I would accept a collect call from a state of Florida correctional institution. It was him! The call had finally come! Nervously, I pressed the number I was instructed to, and I heard Jeff's voice for the first time in over three years.

"Hello, hello?"

I was frozen for a moment, and my voice sounded strange to me when I finally replied, "Hello."

"How you doing, Allen?" Jeff asked me.

"Fine. Good."

The phone got quiet for what seemed to be hours but was only seconds. Then I asked him how he was doing, and he answered that he was OK. While we were talking, I could hear the other inmates, some talking and some screaming. I asked him what was going on in there and what was all the commotion. He told me that using the phone was a privilege and there was always a line. I asked him how he was surviving in there and his voice changed. He said in a very somber tone, "I'm doing the best I can and making the best out of it in here." A few seconds later, he told me his time was up and that he would write again right away and would try to call me again as soon as he could. And just like that, the phone went dead.

I stood there, actually wishing we could have talked a little longer. As I hung up and sat down, I pictured, mostly from TV and movies, what the scene and his situation must have been like there in that prison. The more I thought, my heart began to grieve for him. I had gone from hating him and never wanting to see his face again and trying to have him sentenced to death, to feeling truly sorry for him. Only if I could turn the hands of time back. Only if I would have stayed home. Only if I had sought Jeff mental illness help instead of prison. The only if's sped through my mind often and constantly. I just wanted a do over in life. Even if I personally couldn't have helped Jeff or been there for him, at least I would not have made it my life mission to put him in a place that would only destroy whatever dignity that he had left after what he had done.

As time went by, we would talk more, and he would write more. Most of our conversations were small talk. He would inquire about people from our old neighborhood or tell me who from our old neighborhood he had run across in prison. He wanted to know about me, and he even told me that he had seen me on the news and in the newspaper—articles about the community projects I was involved in. After his initial letter, we never spoke about what happened and what he had done to our mother. It was as if we both knew that was a line we could not cross.

I learned that in our situation, it was best to leave the past and the hurts of the past behind. It was best because the hurt and pain my heart felt when he murdered our mother was so deep that I never thought I would heal. It was a pain that needed to heal. The pain of losing your mother is a pain that is hard to describe. But the pain of your mother being murdered by your own brother, her son, is impossible to describe.

I was finally in a place to realize that Jeff had to be experiencing a similar pain and hurt. He had to be going through the what if's as well. He had to be hurting deep, knowing that our mother was gone forever because of him. Consequently, we were all hurt because of the loss of our mother. This deep agonizing hurt would one day not be as bad, but at that time we all had to navigate through it. And so Jeff and I started communicating more often as time went by. We were building a relationship all over again and it was very clear that this journey would take some time, but finally it had begun. This was unfamiliar territory for all of us. How long would it take to come to a place of acceptance and peace that our mother was gone and we would never see her again? How long would it take to totally heal? How long would it take to totally forgive? How long would it take for Jeff to heal? How long would it take for Jeff to overcome his demons and mental illness?

Unfortunately, there were no answers to any of these questions. It was truly a journey; a journey in the sense that wherever we were going it would truly take time. How much time, no one knew. Journeys are never certain or exact. Journeys are different for different individuals. They are filled with uncertainty. But the good thing about journeys is that they provide perspective, change and growth.

I can remember dreaming one night that my mother was smiling, because all she ever wanted to see was my younger brother and I getting along. I learned that the most important part of the journey to forgiveness was to understand that even though what happened was terrible and horrific, that there is a reason why people do what they do. While it impacted me and my life, and the life of others, too, the real issue was that something was wrong with my younger brother. He was not in his right mind. He was dealing with schizophrenia. He was dealing with mental illness. The journey to forgiveness is all about perspective. Whatever he had done would never be undone, so forgiveness was really all about how I handled what he had done. It was all about me understanding that holding onto anger, hate and rage would only keep me stuck in that time and place that had become a prison for me. Nothing was going to bring my mother back to life, but after releasing the anger, hate and rage I realized that I still had a life to live. We will never be able to completely shield ourselves from harm and pain in life, but what we can do is not allow it to incarcerate us and take away our freedom. I had never sought professional help to deal with my pent-up feelings. All the pain had been stashed in my inner soul. I had imprisoned myself by filling my heart with hate. I had never spoken to anyone about what happened or what I was feeling. It wasn't the best way to handle things, but it was the only way I knew back then.

While I did not seek professional help from a psychologist, therapist, or other trained mental health professional, this is not the path that I would recommend to others. Over the years, and particularly in my role as a senior pastor, counseling with people facing so many different issues, I've learned to appreciate the benefit of relying on such professionals in order to navigate through our emotions and hurt.

The journey to forgiveness starts when we face our pains and disappointments, resolve them as best as possible, and understand that the most important element in the journey to forgiveness is time. Time heals and time mends. During the course of life, we will encounter some bumpy roads, curves, roadblocks and detours, but the essence of life is about embracing the process. The process is essential and

The Freedom of Forgiveness

must take its course. You can't speed it up and you can't slow it down. The process is the process, and it looks different to different people. My journey to forgiveness was a process that was absolutely necessary for me to be totally and completely set free from the prison of unforgiveness.

My younger brother served seventeen years in prison and was released. While our relationship will never be that of normal siblings, it also won't be one filled with hate and anger. Jeff has gone on to live a productive life and is doing very well for himself, considering what he has to live with. He's also involved with helping the homeless. While most of my relatives do communicate with him in some way, including my older brother on occasion, my stepfather has chosen not to have a relationship with him.

And even though Jeff and I live in the same city, my choice not to have a close relationship with him is not based on me still being hurt or angry or hating him. It has everything to do with the fact that my life has gone in a totally different direction, and I have chosen not to live in the past nor be reminded about the past as it relates to him murdering our mother. He's my brother. I haven't abandoned him. I pray for him. I only want what's best for him for the remainder of his life.

But I can't, I just can't – do the Christmas and Sunday - at - the-beach things with him, although I have forgiven him.

The Freedom of Forgiveness

While my life has had its share of challenges, my choice to forgive has allowed me to move on with my life in the things that have brought me fulfillment, peace and joy. As the Senior Pastor and founder of The Ark Church, I have been able to share my story on a regular basis and teach about forgiveness to our congregation and others, because of the experience that I've had. Forgiveness is a process filled with revelation. The beginning of my revelations was Jeff's letter. Forgiveness allows the heart and mind to let go of hurts and offenses and allows a person to experience peace. The process is different for everyone. You should never compare or judge yourself according to someone else's experience. I will not attempt to explain why life deals us tragic experiences, but I do know that my faith in God lead me to a place where even though I didn't understand, I got to a place where I just knew that better days would come if I just kept the faith and continued to live. Learn to live your own process out.

Chapter 8

WHAT FORGIVENESS IS AND IS NOT

Forgiveness is strength retained, but unforgiveness is strength surrendered. Forgiveness means to pardon, to release, to liberate or set free. It means that you forfeit any right you have to hate a person for a previous wrong that they may have committed against you. When Jesus said to love your enemy, He was not only teaching good ethics, but He was also teaching good mental health. Unforgiveness robs a person of their joy, their peace, their wholeness and their soundness of mind. I personally believe that unforgiveness is one of the main reasons for emotional and mental health problems that many people struggle with. It is possible to have a sickness in our body and not even know it, and unforgiveness is like that. We can have it in our hearts and not even realize it.

As I tackle this issue of what forgiveness is, it's important to know some of the signs of unforgiveness being present in our lives. In order for you to truly grasp what forgiveness is, I want to highlight some things you should not do, so that you can avoid being hurt or offended unnecessarily again. Let's take a close look at what forgiveness is not.

FORGIVENESS IS NOT APPROVAL OF WHAT THE OFFENDER DID TO YOU

Sometimes we battle in our minds with the fact that if we forgive, we are approving and accepting of what was done to us. This is not true. Just because we forgive, this doesn't mean that we approve or that we're OK with what was done to us at all. Forgiveness is understanding that perhaps we had no control over what happened to us, but we can control how it affects us. Forgiveness is when we have decided to release hurt or offense as opposed to holding on to it because the person or persons may think that we're OK with what happened.

FORGIVENESS IS NOT CLOSING OUR EYES TO WRONG

Forgiveness does not mean that we do not call wrong, wrong! Forgiveness is not living in denial or pretending that the offense never happened. When we forgive, we don't have to pretend that the offense never happened.

FORGIVENESS DOES NOT MEAN THAT YOU DO NOT REPORT A CRIME

When someone commits a criminal act towards

you, according to the laws of the land, forgiveness is not a refusal to report it. You may decide not to report the crime against you, and that's your prerogative, but you should not make this decision based on the precept of forgiveness, thinking that reporting a crime intercepts forgiveness. For example, a woman gets raped by a relative on a Saturday night. She attends church the next morning broken, hurt and confused. She hears the pastor preach from the pulpit that day that we should forgive anything and all things that people do to us. She leaves the church, and even though she wants to report the rape and she should report the rape, she decides not to because the pastor said to forgive. Yet, even though the bible teaches us to forgive, when someone has committed a crime against you, you still have a right to report that crime, and allow the laws of the land to deal with that person, even if you have forgiven them. The woman in this example should not feel that reporting a crime against her means that she could not or would not forgive, or that she has not already done so.

FORGIVENESS IS NOT MAKING EXCUSES FOR SOMEONE OR COVERING UP FOR SOMEONE WHO HURT YOU

While there was a reason why my brother murdered my mother, in my opinion, there was no excuse. Making excuses or lying about an offense is living in denial. For example, an alcoholic husband consistently physically and verbally abuses his wife. His wife shares the experiences with her best friend, but in doing so, the wife says, "It's because he drinks. Maybe if he didn't drink, he wouldn't beat me." In this instance, the wife may be making excuses for why she is being beat. Most people think that if they forgive the person or persons, that they have to cover up the offense, even lie about it, if someone asks them.

They feel that admitting what someone has done to them is the same as not forgiving. Again, there may be a reason why someone hurt you, but in my view, there is never an acceptable excuse for someone hurting you.

FORGIVENESS IS NOT FORGETTING

Forgiveness is not at all about forgetting what happened to you. Forgiveness is all about not allowing what happened to you to hinder you from moving forward. As a pastor, one of the things that grieves my heart is when people use scripture incorrectly to validate or substantiate their actions when hurting someone. Some people are very quick to say, "If you forgive me then you will forget what I did." In fact, there is a very popular scripture in the bible that many Christians and sometimes even non-Christians like to quote when they offend someone and they want that person not to remember what they did. This scripture is found in Philippians 3:13-14, and it says this:

The Freedom of Forgiveness

"Forgetting what lies behind and straining forward to what lies ahead, I press on toward the goal" (NRSV).

The word "forgetting" in this scripture is not telling or even suggesting that a person mentally or emotionally forget anything in the past. This word forgetting comes from an original Greek word that does not suggest that a person suddenly develops Alzheimer's or blots out of their mind what happened.

Our minds are like computers—they store information, events and especially tragedies. The word forgetting originates from a Greek word meaning barrier, fence or wall. So, what the Apostle Paul is saying in this bible verse is this: We should not allow the past to become a barrier, fence or wall around us, to imprison us mentally, spiritually or emotionally. Such a barrier could keep a person from moving forward in life. So, forgiveness is not forgetting!

FORGIVENESS IS NOT REPRESSION

Forgiveness is not holding the pain inside, hoping and wishing that it will all somehow go away. For years, I held all the pain, hate and anger inside of me, hoping that it would someday go away. It never went away. What I was trying to do, instead of forgiving, is called repression. Repression is the restraint, prevention, or inhibition of a feeling.

Sometimes we choose to repress things that may be uncomfortable to deal with. But that's akin to putting a bandage on a major surgery scar or wound. It really doesn't begin to cover the surface, much less allow for healing.   In order for us to truly forgive, we cannot repress our feelings about the things that have caused us hurt. Instead, we must confront those feelings, deal with them, and release them. Again, we all take different paths to get to this place of release, and ultimately forgiveness. Some may choose to seek professional help through a counselor, pastor, psychologist, or other mental health professional. I highly recommend this, as it creates an opportunity to discuss your feelings openly, usually in a comfortable, non-judgmental environment. Some may choose to talk through the issues with their loved ones – perhaps a spouse or best friend. The truth is, it doesn't matter how you choose to get there, what's important is that you do get there!

FORGIVENESS IS NOT SUBMITTING TO ABUSE

This means that you don't allow people to keep on hurting you over and over again. Many people think that if they forgive someone, they are obligated to continue having the same level of relationship that they had with the person or persons prior to the hurt or offense. This is not true. You can forgive someone and still, because of their habitual and continued abuse, need to withdraw yourself from that person.

Withdrawal means, "I care about you, but I love myself enough to stop being abused mentally, physically, emotionally or spiritually."

FORGIVENESS IS NOT AUTOMATICALLY TRUSTING AGAIN

Forgiveness is a must in order for us to live in freedom, but trust is earned! Forgiveness does not automatically rebuild trust. Trust is rebuilt by accountability and a change in behavior. For example, a woman's husband cheats on her and has sex with another woman outside their marriage. The wife finds out and it crushes her, not to mention that it destroys her trust for her husband. While forgiving her husband is a must, trust has to be earned back by the husband.

Many people think that forgiveness automatically restores trust. They may say, "If you had truly forgiven me, you would trust me again." That's not so. Trust must be earned by a change in behavior and accountability. This may mean that the husband in this example may have to report to the wife about his whereabouts at all times until she feels comfortable and can trust that he is where he says he is. A lot of people get hurt over and over again because they feel that forgiveness automatically means the re-establishment of trust. Listen carefully: We can forgive someone and still not trust them. Trust and forgiveness are two different things. Trust is built on honesty, consistency, predictability and accountability over time. When trust is lost or destroyed, it has to be re-established, and this happens when the person who broke it operates with honesty, consistency, predictability and accountability. Forgiveness is our part and our responsibility to walk in when we have been offended. But the restoration of trust is the others person's part or responsibility.

FORGIVENESS IS NOT ALWAYS RESTORATION OF RELATIONSHIPS

If you think that forgiveness means that you run right back into a relationship that hurt you, then you are sadly mistaken. Forgiveness doesn't mean that you will be automatically reconciled with the person, or that the relationship is automatically restored. Running back into a relationship without certain criteria being met can be devastating, and you could be setting yourself up to be hurt again. Forgiveness may not be immediate or automatic restoration or reconciliation. Sometimes the relationship may never be restored or reconciled. You have forgiven, but you have also chosen to sever the toxic and unhealthy relationship. But, if both the offender and the offended do desire the restoration of the relationship, they must understand the requirements for that restoration. Here are some of them:

- Repentance - This word means "to go in the opposite direction." If the relationship was destroyed by lies, the liar must learn to be truthful. This is possible by changing the way that they think. Meaning that they realize that lying is not acceptable or necessary, and then changing their actions to match.

- Restitution - Restitution means to compensate for loss, damage or injury. The offender must demonstrate a willingness to make things right before you consider restoration of the relationship.

- Accountability - The offender must acknowledge responsibility for the offense and that they are responsible to the person who was offended or hurt.

- Time - I have learned that most things in life can be healed and resolved in time. Time has a way in some cases of accomplishing things that even experts and specialist can't accomplish. Usually, things simply need time to heal before the process of restoration and reconciliation can take place.

- Counseling - The advice, expertise and wisdom of therapist and psychologists should never be taken for granted or minimized. Depending on the offense, the person who committed it may need to seek counseling before reconciliation can take place. If a person refuses to get counseling in a situation that clearly requires it, then it probably isn't time to start the process of reconciliation, much less of restoring the relationship.

FORGIVENESS IS NOT AVOIDING CONFRONTATION

Some people would rather blow off an offense than confront the person who offended them. It's amazing how many people walk around hurt, damaged and offended, but never say anything to the person who hurt them. It is not wrong to confront, but the confrontation should only happen when things have cooled off, when all parties involved agree to reason and discuss, and when emotions and feelings have hopefully healed. While confronting the person or persons who hurt you or offended you may not always be necessary, it is important to understand that confronting them should not be automatically ruled out.

Chapter 9

SIGNS OF UNFORGIVENESS

At this point you may be wondering how much of this book is applicable to you. You know you've been hurt in the past by someone, maybe even by multiple people ...and you don't feel as though it affects your day-to-day life. But you've read some things in this book that pulled at your heart string, or that has caused you to wonder, "Have I truly forgiven?" I want to share with you some things to consider in making this assessment. The truth is, only you can determine, by introspection, whether you have unforgiveness in any area of your life, or toward any particular individual. As you read through this list, I challenge you to be honest with yourself, and to search your heart for the truth of the statements and how they apply to you. Doing so can be the beginning of your life changing journey to forgiveness.

Here are some of the signs that may suggest you have not forgiven someone:

- The inability to hear a person's name without

getting angry. For example, you're at a get together with some friends, and one of them brings up the name of a mutual friend, who happens to have caused you an offense in the past. Although the person's name was brought up in a lighthearted manner, and everyone else is laughing and joking about the topic being discussed, you find yourself feeling upset, unable to join in the laughter and continue in the conversation. Not only are you experiencing anger, but the anger has reached to a degree where you feel like you need to leave.

- The inability to encounter a person publicly or privately without being flooded with all kinds of negative emotions. For example, it may be years after the incident that caused you hurt occurred, but you run into that person in the mall, you become flooded with emotions and the feelings of anger and rage immediately rush back.

- Dwelling on an offense or a past hurt and refusing to release it. Whenever you are constantly thinking about what happened to you and the person that offended you, this experience is likely because you have not truly forgiven. While you may never forget what was done, you must not allow any offence to occupy your thoughts to that degree.

- Allowing negative feelings toward the person

that offended you to persist. Time truly heals. And sometimes it may take a while to forgive.

I cannot determine for anyone the amount of time it should take them to forgive, but I can assure you that getting the proper professional help will likely shorten the time frame.

- Having a cold and icy demeanor towards those who offended you. Whenever you cannot be warm or at least cordial towards someone that offended you, you cease from being the decent human being that you are, allowing the offense to change who you really are.

- Not having any feelings of love or concern for those who hurt you. One way to truly check your pulse when it comes to forgiveness, is to try praying for the one who hurt you. If you cannot pray for them, chances are you have not forgiven them. If you have truly forgiven, you will have genuine feelings of love and concern for the one who hurt you, and likely will be able to pray for the success and well-being of that individual. This does not mean you have to show that love in a manner such that you are spending time with the person - but love in the sense that you wish, hope and believe the best for them.

- Living by generalizations. This is when you start to target or label a group of people a certain way because you were hurt by a person from that group. Your attitude becomes "all" instead of realizing that there are bad apples in every group of people and profession.

- o   All Blacks
- o   All Hispanics
- o   All Whites
- o   All pastors
- o   All men
- o   All women
- o   All police officers

When you start to live a life of generalization, it really causes you to miss out on the beauty of diversity.

- Refusing to admit or acknowledge that there is still hurt in your heart that someone caused you. Refusing to admit that there is still hurt will only prolong your path to freedom. As in most cases when facing challenges in life, admitting that there is a problem is the beginning of experiencing victory.

- Wishing and hoping to see the person or persons that hurt you suffer. Some call it karma and others may simply say "that's what they get because of what they did to me." However it's said or implied, whenever you desire and

The Freedom of Forgiveness

wish harm on the person or persons that hurt you, this may be an indication that you have not forgiven, and it is not a healthy place for you.

- Having thoughts of revenge, including doing harm to the person that offended you. Unlike the prior statement where you wish that something bad would happen to the person that hurt you, unforgiveness can push you to a place where you actually harm or hurt the person that offended you. You should never seek revenge or to harm the person or persons that hurt you. Just know that your freedom is more important than them being hurt.

- Constantly reliving the offense or offenses that have happened to you by telling anyone that will listen to you about what someone did to you. You should understand that repeatedly telling others what happened to you is not beneficial. Not only does it not change what happened to you, but it could actually cause others that you tell to develop ill-feelings toward the offender and become imprisoned by unforgiveness because of you are constantly reliving and telling others about the offense.

- Allowing a past hurt or offense to make you bitter towards someone else who reminds you of the person that hurt you. For example, you may end up having resentment and anger towards a co-worker that reminds you of the person that offended you. At this point you are clearly allowing unforgiveness to control you.

Here are some things to consider as you start, continue or complete your journey to forgiveness and freedom:

- o   Who do I need to forgive?
- o   Who do I need to apologize to?
- o   Who do I need to release?
- o   And who do I need, lovingly and in peace, to confront?

Unforgiveness will keep you living in the past and it will rob you of your now. Life is short and tomorrow is not promised. The reason that it's called the present is because it gives us our now. We can't change yesterday, and we don't have tomorrow yet, but we have now. Now is the time to be free. Now is the time to be happy. Now is the time to enjoy life.

Unforgiveness means that you are nursing a grievance, holding a grudge, and that you have kept a record of wrongs done to you. People all over the world have fought for liberty and freedom; millions of lives have been lost in these wars. But the freedom gained has proven to be worth it. It's worth it because every free nation affords its people the opportunities to be and become all that they can be and want to be. It's time for you to live your life in complete freedom and walk in forgiveness, not for the other person or persons, but for yourself!

BE FREE!

Photo Album

Allen 2 yrs old with Mom

Allen's Prom with Mom

Allen with Daughter

Allen's Mom birthday 1983

Allen with Mom 1989

The Freedom of Forgiveness

My brother Jeff and I March 2, 1997

My brother Jeff and I July 6, 1997

FOR SPEAKING ENGAGEMENTS SEND REQUEST TO:

Allenbjackson@hotmail.com or allenbjackson07@gmail.com

Website: www.Allenbjackson.com

Follow Allen B. Jackson on:

 &

subscribe: to Channel

Subscribe to: "You are a winner" Podcast

www.ingramcontent.com/pod-product-compliance
Lightning Source LLC
LaVergne TN
LVHW050625090426
835512LV00007B/662